A New Day

A New Day

A true story of faith, healing, and miracles

Dora Barilla

Because miracles were meant to be shared

The Terkin Family,

Thank you for your
love and support over
the years

Dora

Stephens Press • Las Vegas, Nevada

Editor: Jami Carpenter
Cover Designer: Sue Campbell
Production Assistance: Scott Harmon
Production Coordinator: Stacey Fott

Photos: pg. 15 Stephens Press photo; pg. 19 Marie Barilla; pg. 26 Dina Harris; pg. 34 Mike Barilla; pgs. 44, 46, 49, 50 Upland Fire Department Personnel; pg. 55 Dora Barilla; pg. 104 Upland Fire Department; pg. 105 Dora Barilla; pg. 106 Walter Richard Weis/Inland Valley Daily
Bulletin; pg. 121 Melanie Barilla; pg. 163 Jack Antonio, Studio 1921; pg. 165 Kelly Dilbeck

Cataloging in Publication
Barilla, Dora.
A new day : a true story of faith, healing, and miracles / by Dora Barilla.
172 p. : photos ; 23 cm.
ISBN: 1-935043-12-9
ISBN-13: 978-1-935043-12-6
Traces the journey of faith and healing after her firefighter husband is critically injured.
1. Barilla, Don. 2. Brain injury-Personal narratives. 3. Fire fighters. Head injuries-Rehabilita-
tion. I. Title.
617.48'1'0443 dc22 2009
2009929631

STEPHENS PRESS, LLC
A Stephens Media Company

Post Office Box 1600
Las Vegas, NV 89125-1600
www.stephenspress.com

Printed in Hong Kong

Families of brain injury patients, may this book fill you with hope.

Rebecca and Catie, never forget the miracle. God is with you regardless of your circumstances. God gave me peace, but both of you gave me courage. I love you, Mom.

Friends, when life gets really difficult, don't jump to the conclusion that God isn't on the job. Instead, be glad that you are in the very thick of what Christ experienced. This is a refining process, with glory just around the corner.
1 PETER 4:12

Despite a devastating lightning strike, towering redwoods have the ability
to recover and thrive. Just like the Barillas, after tragedy struck their family,
they found the will and determination to move beyond their devastation.
Their story represents a journey of finding strength in the midst of a storm.
Now their scars are only a reminder to others that there is not only hope of life,
but abundant life through the grace of God's amazing promise.

Contents

Foreword

FEW THINGS ARE MORE POWERFUL THAN TRUE STORIES. "TESTI-monies," as we call them in church, not only encourage others in their struggles, they build faith and defeat forces that seek to destroy life. The Bible says it like this, *"They overcame him [the enemy] by the blood of the Lamb and **by the word of their testimony**"* (Revelation 12:11).

Tom and Dora's word of testimony demonstrates the kind of faith, hope and love that will inspire, challenge and motivate you to "keep on keepin' on" no matter what life may bring your way. The Barilla's personal journey is no neatly packaged feel good movie of the week which quickly wraps up with a happy ending. Like real life, it is full of ups and downs. But their persistent faith and indomitable spirit turn some of our favorite slogans into reality — setbacks are turned into comebacks; tests become testimonies; and messes are transformed into a message.

Philosophical questions that are academic theory for many become intensely personal, even agonizing, in the face of tragedy. With honest transparency Tom and Dora deal with age old questions like "Why do bad things happen to good people?" How they handle such questions and issues while in the midst of the battle may surprise you. No pat answers, but neither is there unquenchable despair. The Barillas discover that while they may not have all the answers, they know **the Answer**. It is their faith in God and confidence in His ultimate purpose that guides them during the darkest of days.

Your faith and confidence in God will grow as you travel with the Barillas through the valley of the shadow of death. The Barillas, as did the apostle Paul, discovered God the Deliverer in that valley. *"We were under great pressure, far beyond our ability to endure, so that we despaired even of life. Indeed, in our hearts we felt the sentence of death. **But this happened that we might not rely on ourselves, but on God, who raises the dead.** He has delivered us* *from such a deadly peril, and he will deliver us. On him we have set our hope that he will continue to deliver us"* (2 Corinthians 1:8–10, NIV). God never wastes a hurt.

— DR. JIM REEVE
FOUNDING PASTOR,
FAITH COMMUNITY CHURCH

Acknowledgments

First and foremost I thank God for the miracle our family received. I wrote this book to remind the world of His amazing glory, even in the midst of tragedy.

I have an undying gratitude toward those who were faithful and prayed, to the medical community who broke all the rules and allowed us to be by Tom's side 24/7, to the decisive actions of the paramedics, nurses, and surgeons, to those who went to softball games for my girls, for those who held fundraisers, for those who cooked meals, for those who did our lawns, for those who sent cards, for those who stayed with Tom in the hospital, and for those whose shoulders we cried on. You are all the true angels here on earth. The miracle was manifested because people were faithful. Thank you for showing the best in humanity. May God bless each and every one of you. You all showed us the path to healing.

I would also like to thank everyone who encouraged me to write down our story and to those who guided me through the writing and publishing process. Bruce McAllister gave me so many pearls and I will be forever grateful for his wisdom. Dr. Jordan inspired me to share my story with other traumatic brain injury patients and without his encouragement I may never have published our journey. The perspectives from many were shared in this book and I would like to personally thank you all for sharing your hearts with the world. Healing occurred for so many of us and I know how challenging it was for some of you to actually write down your thoughts. I would also like to thank Renate Krause, Carolyn Uber, and Jami Carpenter. You all helped carry me through the writing and publishing process. You were so patient, encouraging, and kind. Thank you Joyce Hopp for the words of wisdom "the only good writing is rewriting"; how true that statement is.

I never would have had the stamina to write our story without the love and support of my husband, Tom, and my two beautiful daughters, Rebecca and Catie. Thank you for allowing me the time to heal through writing. Mom, please know how much I appreciate you reading the story over and over and over again. Thank you to all of my friends and family who viewed the first copy and encouraged me to actually publish it. As much as I appreciate everyone who read it, I am most grateful to Andy Hiben for his review. It meant the world to me.

Last but not least I would like to thank Heather Allen for her friendship and also for helping me to grow in my faith at a very early age. Those whirlybirds for Jesus paid off.

Introduction

Daily Bulletin

TOUR BUS, FIRE ENGINE CRASH; FIREFIGHTER
IN CRITICAL CONDITION
3/16/2005

ONTARIO — One man was killed and a firefighter was left clinging to life after a casino tour bus packed with dozens of passengers collided with a fire engine on the 10 Freeway Tuesday morning.

Upland Fire Department engineer Tom Barilla, 40, who was driving the firetruck, was ejected and suffered major chest and head injuries, according to California Highway Patrol officers at the scene.

With the eastbound 10 at Fourth Street closed down, Barilla was airlifted to Arrowhead Regional Medical Center, where he underwent emergency surgery. He remained in critical condition late Tuesday.

The two other firefighters on the engine sustained minor injuries.

The vehicles collided at about 7:30 a.m. as the Upland fire crew was responding to an earlier accident on the westbound carpool lane of the 10 Freeway.

Barilla, who was headed eastbound on the 10, had planned to park his engine next to the freeway median to gain access to the westbound side and was gradually merging left into the carpool lane, CHP Officer Tony Nguyen said.

The tour bus, driven by 51-year-old Nam Jae Chung of Lakewood, was traveling eastbound in the carpool lane when it collided with the left rear of the engine, causing the engine to rotate counter-clockwise.

The right front of the bus struck the driver's side of the engine, Nguyen said. The engine then veered right, crossing all lanes of the freeway, coming to rest on the right shoulder just west of Fourth Street.

The tour bus came to a stop in the carpool lane. No other vehicles were involved in the crash.

Firefighters were forced to cut through crushed metal to free the panicked bus passengers.

Twenty-six people, including the three Upland firefighters, were taken to Arrowhead Regional Medical Center for treatment.

"(Barilla's) family doesn't want the details of his condition released but I can say he sustained injuries to his chest, face and head," said Dr. Dev GnanaDev, the hospital's medical director.

Mike Barilla, 41, said Tuesday afternoon that his brother Tom was still in intensive care and that the family was waiting.

"He's very critical right now," he said by cell phone Tuesday from Arrowhead Regional.

Mike Barilla said Tom has a wife, Dora, and two young daughters, and has been with the Upland Fire Department for 18 years.

"He comes from a background of firefighters," Mike Barilla said. "My dad was a firefighter, I'm a firefighter in Pasadena and our other brother is a firefighter in Phoenix."

Mike Barilla said his brother is known as the handyman in the family.

"He's always over at my house fixing things," said Mike Barilla, who is a firefighter/paramedic at Pasadena.

GnanaDev said the hospital was put under a code orange alert as a result of the collision.

That firefighter in critical condition was my husband Tom Barilla.

Do miracles still happen? I believe they do. I feel amazingly blessed to have experienced a miracle that was manifested in my life through a tragedy . . .

Human tragedy comes in many forms and it leaves its mark upon those it touches. That mark will be one of desolation or become a building block to a deeper and more meaningful existence here on earth. My father once told me that trials and tribulations were just life's path to growth. I never would have believed that a tragedy would bring me a life with a greater love and passion for everything, but it did. Dad you were right.

We all watched the events of 9/11 and were changed forever. Tragedy can make you stronger and more resilient. Tom used to say that he saw people every day on their worst day. Firefighters are faced with tragedy every day, but as a matter of survival they distance themselves emotionally. But when one of their own falls in the line of duty, the response opens up the emotional floodgates and a reality is uncovered. Years later you still see stickers saying "We will never forget." That saying was proven a reality; firefighters don't forget their fallen.

On March 15, 2005, the Oak Room of Arrowhead Regional Medical Center, with a capacity of 200, was filled with fireman from all regions of southern California. They were there to show support for a fallen firefighter tragically injured on the freeway when struck by a tour bus traveling to a local casino. The vivid images of a demolished fire engine were plastered on every local and national media channel. I wondered why all of these people were there to see Tom. Did Tom know all of these people? No, they were there showing their support because someone in their family was fighting for his life and they were there to offer any gesture they could. Tom's accident represented all of them, a part of the firefighter family. Tom was the fireman on 9/11 that they couldn't help. Tom was each one of them. Each fireman in that room knew it could be any of them at any time lying in a hospital bed fighting for his life, but it just happened to be Tom that day. Tom was the statistic waiting to happen.

In the months following the accident, firefighters from all over the country poured out gestures of love and support to our family. Tom received a hand signed T-shirt from New York firefighters that we hung in his hospital room. The local firefighters stationed near the hospital visited Tom daily with food, support, and well wishes. I was so blessed to witness the incredible bond between fellow firefighters. If the world were more like the brotherhood of the fire service, it would be a much better place.

Our family was given a miracle. Tom survived against all odds. The power of prayer, community, and prompt emergency medical attention worked together and restored Tom back to health.

The human body has an amazing ability to heal. We are not only physical beings; we have emotional and spiritual components. Healing has many aspects and can be accomplished through faith, love, and support. Tom suffered a traumatic brain injury along with multiple chest and facial injuries. I was told his chances of survival were minimal and if he did survive the results would be devastating. No one expected him to live, let alone make a full recovery and return to work in six months. Though Tom was the only one who was physically injured, our family was healed through Tom's accident.

Chapter 1: *The Accident*

We are hard pressed on every side, but not crushed,
perplexed but not in despair, persecuted, but not
abandoned; struck down but not destroyed.
2 CORINTHIANS 4:8

KFROG — MORNING TRAFFIC REPORT
There has been a serious accident on the 10 freeway eastbound on
Fourth Street involving a fire truck. Traffic is backed up for miles,
folks, and it doesn't look like it will be moving for a while.

GROWING UP IN LOS ANGELES, YOU BECOME ACCUSTOMED TO TRAF-fic reports on the radio and immune to the details of a fatal accident on the freeways. Honestly, after such reports my thoughts would be on an alternative route to my final destination. Little did I know that this particular traffic report on the local radio station would be the one that changed my life forever.

Knowing this location was the city next to my husband's fire department, I became concerned for the poor firemen in Ontario who may have been affected by this accident. After all, things like that never happen to you, only someone else. A phone call to Tom was in order. I tried the fire station on my cell phone as I was pulling up the hill to Loma Linda University. I quickly received an answer, "Upland Station One; Captain Mensen."

"Hi, Steve. Could I please speak to Tom?"

Steve struggled to respond to my simple request. "Dora, I meant to call you, but I didn't have any information. Did someone tell you to call?"

I asked Steve what he was talking about.

Steve blurted out, "They have been in an accident and I don't have any of the details." It was at that point the numbness began. "Dora, please give me a number where you can be reached and I will call you as soon as I know something."

We both hung up and I walked into the school in a daze, feeling an emptiness that overcame me like a sudden hurricane that desolates a town in an instant. Statistics were the last thing on my mind, although I had arrived early to do last minute studying for my exam. I walked into the first open door with a familiar face. Dr. Naomi Modeste looked at me and questioned what was wrong. I could only respond with, "I don't know, but my husband was . . ."

My cell phone rang; it was a division chief with the Upland Fire Department. "Dora, is there someone there I can talk to?" were the first words I heard. I handed the phone to Dr. Modeste and began thinking of the years I have spent in hospitals, the countless times I had witnessed or heard about the communication vine when loved ones had passed on. I reviewed the protocol in my head: 'Don't tell the loved one directly; make sure someone is there to support them.'

My numbness turned to shock and then to disbelief. This couldn't happen to Tom; he was the safest fireman in the world. This only happened to other people. How was I going to tell the children? Was I dreaming? The thoughts were random and uncoordinated, but it was better than thinking about what the person on the other line was saying to Dr. Modeste. When I came back to reality, I was handed the phone and told that Tom was airlifted to Arrowhead Regional Medical Center and I needed to get there as soon as possible. After my break with reality and what I had imagined, I was relieved, figuring that Tom was alive or they would not have airlifted him to the hospital.

I hung up, Dr. Modeste grabbed her keys, and we drove to the hospital, though that five-mile drive took over an hour. With southern California traffic anything is possible, so it never occurred to me that the congestion on the 10 freeway was due to the horrific accident involving my husband.

What do you talk about on the drive to the hospital when you are given this type of news? We didn't talk; we prayed. Dr. Modeste prayed for God to come and comfort me and heal Tom. This was the first of many prayers that would follow and set the stage for coping with this enormous tragedy my family was about to face. My type "A" personality kicked in and I began thinking of tasks I could complete, as I had little control over the current situation with my husband in critical condition and me stuck on the freeway in traffic.

I took out my cell phone and began making phone calls while Dr. Modeste began to strategize alternate routes to the hospital. Who do I call? I needed prayer and called my long time friend, Renee Tullar, and asked her to put an urgent prayer request on the email at our church. Knowing few details at the time, my request was simply to please pray for Tom, who had been in accident. My second phone call was to Tom's brother, Mike, the rock of his family. Mike was Tom's best friend, brother, mentor, and the person I knew Tom would want to be notified first.

Mike is a fireman with the Pasadena Fire Department and encouraged Tom to get into the fire service. Tom has five siblings, four brothers and a sister. Mike is the closest in age and lives only five miles from Tom and me. Yes, Mike would be the next phone call. Melanie, his wife, answered the phone and I told her that Tom had been in an accident and had been airlifted to Arrowhead Regional Medical Center and that she and Mike needed to come.

Being a fireman, Mike knows tragedy all too well. Words do not need to be spoken; he knows when someone is airlifted to the trauma center and not the local

Tom and his brother Mike playing firefighters as children in New York.

hospital, the injuries are serious. I didn't have time for additional details because our phone call was lost.

Mike wasn't able to reach me on my cell phone and called the hospital. For some unknown reason, he reached the emergency department nurse and explained that he was the brother of the fireman they just brought in. She told Mike that he needed to get to the hospital and soon. Mike and Melanie were on their way. In the meantime, I tried to contact someone in my family but I couldn't reach anyone, so I left a message with my grandmother.

MIKE BARILLA:

That morning I was in a state of disbelief. My brother in an accident? No way. But as the telephone call continued, I knew something was not right. My disbelief turned into anxiety and increased into fear. What was going on? After calling the hospital, I was told Tom had been in an accident and was airlifted to the emergency room at Arrowhead Regional Medical Center. Hearing the nurse crying on the phone left me with no feelings at all; my heart sank. My wife and I got into the car and began a trip that took forever. I knew what being airlifted to a hospital meant. Tom had serious injuries. My anxiety now was turning into survival mode. What about the kids? What about Dora? God! Melanie and I could not believe what was happening or what we would be facing when we arrived at the hospital. I began making phone calls while we drove.

Dr. Modeste had exited the freeway and headed down side streets to the hospital. It finally hit me that my husband was being taken to the county hospital. I was petrified. I had spent my entire career improving the policies within our healthcare system and knew the down side to healthcare far too well. My last phone call was to Eric Frykman, the county health officer. I wanted to plead with him to make sure that my husband was well cared for. Eric was a good friend and the only person I could think of who was connected to the county hospital. His wife happened to be having a baby that day and Eric wasn't available. Tom was in God's hands.

We finally arrived at the hospital and walked into the emergency room looking for anyone to give me information about my husband. There were no familiar faces, only a room filled with people needing health care. The security guard in the emergency room was given orders to keep everyone out as the hospital had gone into disaster mode. Again, I did not realize that the multiple injuries causing the disaster were from the accident on the freeway involving my husband. I tried to explain to the security guard that my husband was the firefighter airlifted to the ER. This security guard was unmoved by the information and was adamant about following protocol not to let anyone inside the ER.

There was no phone reception in the ER, so I had to step outside to call someone to help me. I felt so alone; I needed someone to tell me what was going on. I continued to lose phone reception and sat on the step outside and cried out to God to help me. Two young girls, with multiple piercings and tattoos everywhere, came and sat down next to me. They shared with me that God is capable of all things and began to pray with me. Their prayers brought me such comfort. I finally regained my composure and thanked them for their kindness.

You never know who God is going to use when you cry out for His help. I always believed there were angels among us, but honestly I had a different visual. A lesson can be learned in the most interesting of situations. I also realized the impact that a simple kind gesture can make in the midst of a personal tragedy.

A phone call was futile, so I went back into the ER. Dr. Modeste had been trying to get some information and persuade the rigid security guard to let me in to see my husband, to no avail. I stood there in a chairless emergency room shaking so intensely I found it difficult to stand. I began to plead with the security guard for information about my husband. With no results, I opted for a second chance at a phone signal. God must have heard my prayers as I received a signal and called the fire station pleading for help. They were appalled that I had not been given any information and said they would make a phone call.

At that moment Mike and Melanie walked up and embraced me. It is amazing how a familiar face is so important in the midst of crisis. We regained composure and walked into the ER together, determined to find out information about Tom. Mike was not about to let a security guard keep him from his brother and got the security guard's attention with a few firm words. One minute later, the double doors of the emergency room swung open and the firm authority of men in uniform, the Upland Fire Department, grabbed my arm and whisked me back into the emergency room, but not before a sweet young woman grabbed my hand and told me that she was praying for my husband. Another kind gesture that carried me through the next round of information I was about to receive.

I don't remember who else was with the division chief from Upland, because their faces were not familiar to me. All I can remember is seeing the face of Lou Steslicki, a division chief who had made his way through the ranks of the fire service. It had been years since we had socialized with Lou, but I remembered the times we had gone to parties together, laughed, and talked about life. The other firefighters with him were new or I had never spent time with them. Their faces were unknown. The Upland Fire Department had recently hired a new fire chief and even his face was unfamiliar. Having relationships with your coworkers developed a new meaning that day.

MIKE BARILLA:

We arrived at the hospital to find Dora lying on the ground outside the ER *crying; both Melanie and I thought Tom was dead. All I could think about at this time was how thankful I was that Melanie was with me so she could support Dora. I entered the* ER *waiting room to find the place locked down. After speaking to a security guard, my survival mode began to turn into anger. Why couldn't they tell me about my brother? I refused to believe that they couldn't bring Dora to see Tom or back to the doctors who could tell her what was happening with Tom.*

I thought I was being brought back to see Tom, but instead, I was ushered into a private room with a team of counselors. My mind turned back to protocol when family members are notified about the death of loved ones. Why was everyone coming up and giving me their business cards and consoling me like a widow? I felt like a deer in the headlights. Everyone was coming at me and I couldn't move. I tried to make sense of what was happening to me, but I couldn't even comprehend the reality of my situation. In the hour or so I sat in that room, I managed to meet the president of the hospital, the new fire chief, a team of counselors, along with thirty other individuals whose names or titles I cannot recall. I just wanted to see Tom.

No one wanted to tell me they didn't think Tom was going to live, but I could see it in their eyes. They knew that I needed some support and made their best attempts at offering it to me. I must have been talking about my faith in God at one point, because a firefighter asked if he could pray with me. We prayed together and asked God for his peace and to heal Tom. I was getting anxious at this point and needed someone who could give me the answers I needed and I asked the chief to page Tom's best friend, a fellow firefighter, Ed Weaver. I needed Big Ed.

He walked in the room two minutes later. Little did I know, Ed had been walking the hallways of the ER demanding information about Tom. Ed's presence and strength was another answer to my prayers before we were shuffled into another room, bigger, but with fewer people joining me: Dave, my friend Renee's husband, and Lisa Cascadden, the wife of the fire captain in the accident with Tom. I didn't know much about who was hurt or to what extent and I still had little, if any, information about Tom's condition. Though the room was very large, it felt like the white walls were closing in on me.

I sat in this large room with Lisa. Lisa and Joel Cascadden had lost their twenty-one-year-old son eight years ago to a traffic accident. Could God be so cruel to take Tom? Joel had been Tom's captain for over ten years and Tom was like a son to Joel. Joel and Lisa Cascadden were like family. This reality seemed crueler than my mind could comprehend. At this point I began experiencing a serious disconnect with reality. It was surreal. Every moment seemed to bring increasing tragedy. What happened that morning of March 15, 2005? My life was changed forever.

MIKE BARILLA:

As we stood in the room we were bombarded with hospital personnel, but no doctors or nurses telling us about Tom; anxiety began to set in. Finally, we were told he was going to X-ray. Tom was alive! The doctors brought Dora and me into a room and told us that Tom's condition was serious and unstable. Tom could die at any moment. Every moment he lived was a good sign. My feelings now were back in survival mode. I took all emotions and put them behind me; Tom, Dora, and the kids came first. Once again I thanked God Melanie was with me. Having her there allowed me to cope and survive.

More and more familiar faces began to come into the ER but it didn't seem to faze me at all. At this point, God began to carry me, because my body and mind found it difficult to comprehend the information. It is often said that in crisis people go into denial to handle the situation. Denial was my reality at this point. I had been with Tom since I was eighteen years old and we had been married for fourteen years. I had grown accustomed to the reality that things did not exist until I shared them with Tom. I couldn't share this with Tom; therefore it was not real. I could feel Tom's pain and I wanted to die along with him. I began to plead with God for Tom's survival. Please God, heal Tom. Don't let him die. I need him.

The more people who seemed to show up, the less information I received. If the strategy was to "keep Dora occupied until we could tell her Tom was dead," it wasn't working.

Please God, let me see my husband. If he is going to die let me say goodbye, let me kiss him goodbye, let me know he knows Jesus and will be in heaven. Please don't leave me in this large white room without any information.

Finally a doctor arrived. Tom's brother, Mike, and I were taken into a room where we were told that Tom suffered severe injuries and they had difficulty getting Tom to breathe, as both of his lungs collapsed from the trauma to his chest. That was not the worst part. Tom had suffered a severe head injury; the bleeding was significant and they needed to remove a part of Tom's skull. Could I please consent to the surgery?

The doctor had a phenomenal bedside manner, but I struggled to understand the severity of the situation. Did I have a choice? Of course do the surgery! I don't even recall if I asked the right questions, but both Mike and I agreed that this was the only alternative at the time. Removing part of the skull would allow the brain to swell and decrease the inner cranial pressure. Fortunately for us, one of the best neurosurgeons in the region, Dr. Javed Siddiqi, was in the ED that morning and he was available to perform the surgery.

By the way, had Tom ever mentioned a mass on his adrenal gland? His injuries were extensive. He had two crushed lungs, abdominal bleeding, and his face was completely fractured. An invasive emergency airway had been performed in the field. The doctors left the room to perform the extensive surgery. I finally had some information; Tom was alive, but what was really left of him.

That morning Tom was wearing the light blue cotton shirt I bought him for Christmas and his infamous 501 jeans. He always changed into his uniform when he arrived at work. I was wondering what he was wearing now. If I walked down the halls, would I see his blue shirt or did he have time to change into his uniform before the call? I didn't want to picture what he was going to look like; I just wanted to picture him normal.

I was told I could see Tom before they brought him into surgery. Finally; thank God. I was brought through the emergency room where I saw Joel in one of the beds. Joel had suffered serious facial injuries. His face was badly bruised and he had over 150 stitches near his eye. The intensity of the situation began to weigh on me. He held me in his arms crying and stating that he was so sorry. His hug was strong and full of terror, yet I could feel a glimmer of hope. I told Joel that he would be okay; I could just feel it. Joel's face said otherwise. It was a sobering experience to see a strong, grown fireman cry. I told him I was going to see Tom before he went into surgery. He prepared me for a sight that might not resemble Tom.

JOEL CASCADDEN (TOM'S FIRE CAPTAIN):

Tom is not dead, but I don't believe he will survive. What will I say at his funeral? I just can't believe this is happening. I can't bear it. When I see Dora, my heart breaks. I didn't keep her husband safe; all I can do is hold her, cry, and say I'm sorry. At this point, nobody knows Tom's status. I know, though, it is the worst; I've seen these types of injuries before. Survival is unlikely and undesirable. Brain injuries are not like broken bones. If life continues, it is ruined.

My worst nightmare had happened. A member of my fire crew was gone, missing, disappeared. When I woke up after being knocked unconscious, that's what I realized. I don't know what happened, but I knew it was bad, really bad. My fireman, John, was yelling something from the back of the fire engine and a cop was standing in front of the fire engine yelling something. Looking to the left, the driver's door was gone and so was Tom. There was a tour bus across the freeway with the front end torn off. Did that hit us? Climbing out through the now-missing windshield and walking around to the left side of the engine, I saw what could only be described as my worst nightmare. A member of my crew was hurt badly, maybe dead. And it was Tom.

Tom and I are co-workers, but he is my friend, too. Tom is everyone's friend. He was in a pool of blood, but alive. My fireman and a cop were with him helping him breathe, but it was not good. I've seen this kind of injury before; it's the kind you don't survive, a head injury. He's dead, I thought, he's dead. We were trying to help him breathe, but it wasn't working. God, I felt so helpless. John was working on Tom frantically. The cop and I tried to help. Tom wasn't breathing . . . then they came, help came, gently pushing us aside, to help Tom. The helicopter landed and took Tom away. In the hospital, I found Dora, and the tears flowed. I didn't know what to say other than, I'm so sorry. The guilt was overwhelming. I had allowed Tom to get hurt. We were going to have a firefighter's funeral and I would suffer the guilt of survival.

The sight of a trauma patient can be devastating. When they rolled him by in the gurney, I saw an unconscious person that couldn't be my husband. Although I knew it was Tom because of his hair color and general body frame, and sensing his presence, it did not look like my husband. He was bloody and his face and head were so swollen he was unrecognizable. I didn't know where to touch him or where to kiss him. He was rolled out on a stretcher with tubes coming out of just about every location of his

Tom and Dora, April 4, 1992

body. Although he was unconscious, I kissed him and told him God was with him, he was going to be okay, and that I loved him. This was all I had time for because they whisked him off to surgery.

JOHN RUPPERT (TOM'S FIREMAN):

X-rays, CT scans, IVs, blood work, poking, prodding, palpating. "How is Tom?" I would ask. Nobody could answer. I was on the hospital bed, being rolled to another machine for more tests. I passed by Joel standing in the hallway with his wife, Lisa. "How are you doing, John?" Joel asked. His head was wrapped up like a giant Q-tip, face all swollen, but he was standing and walking on his own. That was a good thing to see. There were hundreds of questions, but no answers. All the Upland firemen came to see me, to see how I was doing. I felt fine, I felt sick. We all silently wondered . . . is Tom alive?

The collection of family and firefighters were brought into a waiting room outside of the ICU. It was surreal; I was completely numb at this point and the waiting began for the first of many surgeries. The room was filled with firemen. They were my angels sent to carry me through the fire.

Chapter 2: *Denial*

O FTEN I THINK OF THAT MORNING AS A REMINDER TO ALWAYS SAY I love you and to never hold a grudge for the irritating idiosyncrasies of your loved ones. As I sat and waited for Tom, all I could think about were the things he did that drove me crazy and how I prayed God would give him back to me to continue to drive me crazy.

Tom came out of surgery later that afternoon. They immediately brought him to the ICU on the second floor of Arrowhead Regional Medical Center. The waiting room was filled with family and friends. I was sitting in the waiting room trying to deal with the reality of the situation. By now both Tom's family and mine had been notified, though earlier I had been unable to reach my mom. She had gone to a doctor's appointment and hadn't told anyone. When she finally arrived I was so relieved. I needed my mom. I had friends who worked at one of the local hospitals who also knew where my mother lived. They had posted someone outside of her apartment and the moment she arrived, whisked her to the hospital to be by my side.

JEANNE NASH (DORA'S MOM):
My neighbor had left a note on the elevator and she told me Tom had been in an accident and they didn't think he was going to make it. All the way to the hospital I prayed for Tom, Dora, and the girls. What would they do without him? The family room was full of people; some I knew, some I didn't. I didn't know what to say to Dora or how to tell her how sorry I was that this was happening to her. They took me to see Tom; he looked so bad, and I wouldn't have even known him. Looking at him I asked God to help us all, to make it through this horrible time, and please, Lord, be with my child; she needs you.

When they brought Tom to the ICU we were able to visit him for a few moments at a time. The first time I walked into the room I felt as though I was going to faint. This could not be my husband. The room was so bare. It was sterile and cold. I was so afraid. I wanted to touch him, but there wasn't anywhere to touch. He was so bruised and battered. The unbelievable trauma he had experienced left him unrecognizable. I couldn't breathe; I needed to leave. The pain was more than I could bear. This could not be happening. The love of my life was gone. My optimism turned to desolation. I returned to the waiting room.

JOHN RUPPERT:

I met Tom's brother, Mike, and he took me and a firefighter, Dennis Weaver, into Tom's room in the ICU. I took one look at Tom's face and had to turn away. I broke. He looked worse now at the hospital than he did on the freeway after the accident. His body was limp and lifeless. His face was swollen beyond recognition; he had tubes going everywhere, and there were machines pumping air, blood, fluids, and medicine in and out of his body. I buried my face into Mike's neck and sobbed.

To see Tom that way, helpless and barely hanging on to life, was just too much for me to handle. That was not the Tom I knew. Even to this day, when I think of a fire department, I think of Joel Cascadden and Tom Barilla. To me, Joel Cascadden is everything a fire captain should be, and Tom is a firefighter's firefighter. Tall, strong, smart, problem-solver, quick witted, and the undisputed "king of the one-liners." Everything that I had learned up till that point, I had learned from Joel and Tom. My first few training days as a reserve were with Joel and Tom. My first medical aid traffic accident and fire as a Reserve were with Joel and Tom. My first real structure fire as a professional, paid firefighter was with Joel and Tom. Tom taught me how to do a DL-170, how to drive a fire engine, how to sharpen an axe correctly, and most importantly, how to be a fireman. I looked up to him and wanted to be the type of fireman that he was.

There were so many people. There was nowhere for me to regain my composure. I sat in a room full of people and was completely alone. I remember just staring into space and nodding and smiling when people talked to me. The faces of those who returned from visiting Tom's room would haunt me. I couldn't bear my circumstances. The first seventy-two hours would be critical. I felt the battle in my gut. The glimmer I once had left my body. Who was I kidding? Tom was not going to live and if he did there wouldn't be much left.

Denial can be a very effective tool in handling trauma. I remember sitting in the waiting room pretending like it wasn't me people were coming to console. It was someone else. I had spent my whole life in hospitals; I saw people suffer all the time. I would feel empathy for their situation, but until this moment I could never understand how they really felt. Where do I begin processing all of the challenges I was about to face? I liked denial; it was working well for me.

What was I going to tell my children? I didn't even know what to tell myself. I suddenly became exhausted and at moments I couldn't breathe. I felt physically present in the situation but mentally absent. I didn't have the energy to greet the people who came to see Tom. I am sorry if I was rude to anyone, I just didn't have the strength to be social. I remember so many people in the room and I wanted to scream but it would be so inappropriate. My two best friends drove me home that night to change my clothes and tell my children. I remember on the way back to the hospital being unable to breathe. My friend Renee put her hand on my shoulder and began to pray for peace to overtake my body. I remember feeling peace and an almost disconnect from my body. People told me later that when they came to see Tom they were shocked at how composed I was and that I ended up encouraging them. I had to laugh when I heard this and knew that it could only be God working through me, because at that moment I was a complete mess.

The hospital waiting room became a sleeping area for about fifty family, friends, and firemen. Someone set up a bed for me in the waiting room so I could try to rest, but I did not sleep for three days. I was afraid if I fell asleep, Tom might die and I wouldn't be there to say goodbye. I remember lying there in the dark on the third night and beginning to hyperventilate. The crowd had left for the night and the denial began to wear off. Again the realization of what was happening to Tom began to set in. I had three of Tom's closest friends rush to my side and struggle to console me. They were suffering themselves and they struggled for the words, but their kindness and presence was enough to get me to start breathing again. That was a tough night. The hospital team performed neuro checks every hour to see if Tom would respond to commands or to light. Every time he didn't respond I felt a sinking in my heart. I felt like I was dying along with him. I could feel his pain.

JOHN RUPPERT:
The next few days were horrible. Everybody was there, supporting Dora and her family, filling up the family waiting room to capacity. I was there, waiting also . . . surrounded by everyone, but feeling completely alone. I had less than a year on the job, a rookie. I did not know any of the firemen's wives or families, and they did not know me. I barely even knew the names of my coworkers. I was not on a first-name basis with very many of them. I did not know Tom very well either; I had only been with him and Joel full time for the last three months. I felt like an outsider, like a recently-traded ball player to the Lakers just months before . . . when the team was struck with tragic news that Chick Hearn had just died. Tom was not dead yet. His likelihood of survival was slim, and who knew what would be left of him if he did survive.

I did not like being there at the hospital. I did not know what to do, what to say, how I could help. I met Dora briefly before the accident. I would not have recognized her at the hospital if she would not have been completely surrounded, crying and embracing everyone. What should I say to a woman I did not know, who might have just lost her husband? She has two little girls who had no idea of the severity of the situation.

The first time he gave us thumbs up during his routine neuro check the crowd cheered, the news went up on the website, and the chain of phone calls and emails went out fast and furious. This was the first sign of hope. His brain wasn't dead; he was responding to commands. Thank you, Jesus. The first seventy-two hours felt like an eternity. He was so injured and most people didn't think he would survive. You could see it in the nurses' faces. I refused to believe he was going to leave me here on earth. My growing faith must have seemed humorous to some, but I had to believe.

MIKE BARILLA:

The first four days were a roller coaster of feelings — sadness, anxiety, fear, and helplessness — but something struck me during this time; we never lost hope. No one ever said good bye to Tom. Tom's recovery continued to be a roller coaster of events. Not knowing how much he would recover, if he would be able to return to work, or if he would have a normal life with his family was overwhelming at times. But through faith, prayer, and a whole lot of help from family and friends, we made it through the struggles and emotional drain.

After three days of not sleeping, someone insisted that I at least go home for a few hours to get a little sleep. I remember calling his nurse every two hours to check on his condition. I was so afraid to leave him. That night at three a.m. I fell to my knees at the side of my bed and I cried out to God. "God, please heal Tom," and sobbed in absolute fear. A warmth consumed my body like I had never experienced before in my life. I felt God saying, "Dora, stop asking me to heal Tom and start praising me for healing Tom."

I equate this experience to people talking about finding the Lord. I was raised a Christian so I never experienced the moment that I found Jesus; I never remember a time that Jesus was not in my life. At this moment I had never felt closer to the Lord in my life. I held onto that moment and stood on the word that I believe God gave me. To this day I hold on to that moment and know that must be a fraction of what it will feel like to be in the presence of God. Complete peace.

My denial turned to faith and believing the unseen. I began to speak God's words and it must have worked, because that night the second round of Tom's surgeries began. Removal of his skull to relieve the intercranial pressure was the most life-threatening injury. Now that they believed he was going to live they would move onto his le forte 1 fracture, fractured zygomatic arch on both sides of his face, and insert a permanent tracheotomy. In layman's terms, his jaw was fractured and they basically had to rebuild his face. This surgery was far less stressful than the first and lasted half the time they anticipated.

I hated the term permanent tracheotomy. Did this mean Tom would have a permanent tracheotomy? It was explained that the needle crych performed in the field would be replaced with a tracheotomy. It didn't occur to me that Tom was so critical that he still was breathing through the tube they placed in his throat on the freeway. I was also expecting Tom to be terribly bruised and disfigured after his surgery. The plastic surgeons at Arrowhead Regional Medical Center were exceptional. Apparently this type of surgery can be performed through the mouth. Tom's mouth was already so disfigured it hardly looked like he had surgery at all.

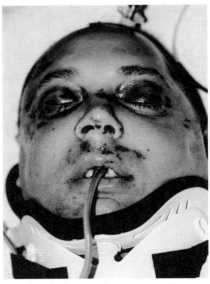

Tom's brothers took a picture of Tom at day eight of his coma. They knew that Tom would want to see what he looked like when he recovered.

He was lucky he was still in a coma at this point, because the metal bars they had to place in his mouth looked like a form of torture. They had also pulled out his last remaining front tooth, so he was toothless. After his second surgery, I began cleaning the blood from the rest of his body. He was more stable and I wasn't afraid to touch him. It was a turning point and I finally had hope that he was going to make it and other people believed he was going to live as well.

One of Tom's nurses had an injury himself several years ago and obviously shared my faith. He would tell me every day what I needed to pray for. At first it was that his inter-cranial pressure would subside, then it was for his lungs, and finally to pray against infection. Several years later, that same nurse told me that he did not believe Tom was going to survive during those first seventy-two hours. People don't survive the type of trauma he experienced. He told me he, too, was inspired by the prayers and support that surrounded Tom.

The days that followed were exhausting, and each day had its pluses and minuses. His healing was not a linear process.

Chapter 3: *The Media*

Do not be anxious about anything, but in everything, by prayer
and petition, with thanksgiving, present your requests to God.
And the peace of God, which transcends all understanding,
will guard your hearts and your minds in Christ Jesus.
PHILIPPIANS 4:6–7

*A*FTER A FEW DAYS IN THE HOSPITAL, I BEGAN TO WONDER HOW this all happened in the first place. How does a bus hit a fire engine? It is pretty hard to miss. The fire department did a pretty good job of hiding all of the newspaper articles from me and quite honestly, at the time I didn't want to know the details. I did see a news clip one day in the hospital, but it was Tom's brother, Mike, at a press conference asking everyone to pray.

The media hounded our family after the accident. My mom told me that the phone rang constantly the day after the accident and the media swarmed the hospital. There happened to be a new media relations person at Arrowhead Regional Medical Center at the time of Tom's accident and I felt like he became one of my best friends. He was so considerate of my feelings and protected me from the media at all costs. I never saw or talked to a reporter until weeks after the accident.

The first day of the accident the hospital asked what we wanted to say to the press and I thought of a grandmother of a captured soldier who I saw on CNN years ago. She was asked what people could do for her and she asked them to pray. I remember praying for their family and was inspired by the woman's faith. Everyone was asking what they could do for me and I asked them to pray. I never had the energy to attend any news conferences so I asked Mike to represent our family and speak to the press. I knew Tom would want Mike to be the spokesperson for the family. I asked Mike to ask people to pray for Tom. What was going to be the thirty-second sound bite in the evening news? Why not, "Could you pray for Tom?" I never expected that to be the clip the media ran over and over. He asked them to pray and that is what the news put as a sound bite. This gave me such comfort. The clips on TV were asking the world to pray. It was amazing how people responded. I still have people tell me, "I prayed for your husband." My response was always the same: "Thank you, it worked."

After two weeks of being isolated, the fire chief came to see me at the hospital and asked if I might consider talking to the press. I said that I would and he connected me with a local reporter for the *Daily Bulletin*, Edward Barrera. He called me that day and asked if he could visit me at the hospital. We met the Saturday before Easter. I had brought the girls in to see their father for a few minutes each day and they happened to be with me that day. The reporter brought a photographer who asked if he could take a picture of Tom. It made me a little sick and I refused the request. Tom looked awful and no one should have to see that. I really liked the reporter, though. I knew he had a story to write, but he was very respectful. We actually went on to do several articles with the same reporter. I think he grew to really care about Tom and told me that he was going to have to excuse himself from any further articles because he could no longer be biased. He went on to another paper a year later and the local articles dwindled. A few articles appeared on the anniversary of the accident, but they were fewer and farther in between. Several national media outlets contacted us, but we ended up refusing interviews because of the pending legal actions.

Chapter 4: *Details of the Accident*

*He gives strength to the weary and increases the power of the
weak. Even youths grow tired and weary, and young men
stumble and fall; but those who hope in the LORD will
renew their strength. They will soar on wings like eagles; they
will run and not grow weary, they will walk and not be faint.*
ISAIAH 40:29-31

FIRE DISPATCH TAPES MARCH 15, 2005

Ontario 161, Ontario 161, Ontario 161: *We've been in a TC. Ontario 161, we've been in a TC. Fourth and the I-10, fourth and the I-10. 161.*

Ontario Medic Engine 161: *I've got an engine . . . my engineer is injured, I am injured, I think my fireman is okay. I need some . . . uuh . . . some help here. Code 3.*

Dispatcher: *Just confirming east or west.*

Ontario Engine 161: *I have an engine on scene now; start another one. Eastbound at Fourth.*

Ontario Engine 135: *Is on scene. We are going to take this to Tac 3.*

Ontario Engine 161: *Send some administrative folks from Upland; we have injured personnel.*

Ontario Medic Engine 135: *This is freeway command; we need an airship for a fireman.*

THANK GOD THE CALIFORNIA HIGHWAY PATROL (CHP) HAD ALready ordered an airship and it was in commute by the time Ontario Fire Department had placed the order. I was told that Mercy Air was in the area and had the helicopter landed, Tom loaded, and in route to Arrowhead Regional Medical Center within six minutes.

To this day, Tom has no recollection of the accident. He lost about a month of his life, at least as far as his memory is concerned. I think that is God's way of protecting people from trauma. I couldn't imagine having to recall the accident from Tom's perspective. When I see the fire engine, I feel ill. It is literally mangled and in pieces. The cab is completely destroyed with the door ripped off and the steering wheel bent in half. How Tom survived I will never understand. That morning the fire reserve who was supposed to sit in the seat behind Tom was running late and never made it to the call. Anyone sitting behind Tom would not have survived. Whatever made him late turned out to be a blessing that morning.

I was not told about the details of the accident until much later. The lawyers told me the less I knew the better. It didn't really matter while Tom was in a coma, but as he began to recover I found myself increasingly interested in the details.

I was told that Tom was entering the high occupancy vehicle lane to respond to a call and was hit by a speeding casino tour bus. It seemed pretty clear-cut to me, but apparently lawyers felt they could distort the truth and make it seem as though Tom was somewhat at fault, so I had to be careful with whom I spoke. I was also told that the bus driver tried to flee the scene, that passengers had commented that the bus driver had said, "If we don't get around this accident, we will be stuck here all day," and that passengers were angry when they were taken to the hospital instead of the casino. None of that mattered after people realized there was money to be made in a lawsuit. It was now about the money and the truth was out the window. Those comments never made it to a deposition.

Anyone can make an assessment as to what happened that morning on the freeway, but I have chosen to believe only those who were at the scene. Opinions were found to be a dime a dozen after the accident. I found the opinions of those who were not at the scene to be worthless.

One source who had a perfect view of the accident was in the first car stopped on the freeway.

Taken from the deposition of the eyewitness:
Well, when I first heard the siren, we were already slowing down, and I didn't hear the siren anymore. But as we were just moving slowly, because everyone was coming to a stop, I saw the lights to my right through the windshield. So I slowed down, which everyone else

did, and then moved a little at a time, as the lights moved forward. I saw the fire truck. It was at a stop, and then it would move a little bit, and then it was at a stop again, just slowly inching over to the carpool lane. I noticed an accident on the opposite side of the freeway that the fire truck was trying to get to. And so I just looked at it, as it moved, stopped, and moved again. The driver kept looking out his window, looking as he kept taking one lane at a time. Then he was in front of me; I saw him looking. As he would look, I would look in my rear view mirror, and I could see cars coming to a stop, and I would look at him, and he would slowly keep moving and he would look again. Then I saw the bus coming on my side-view mirror, not stopping. I was looking at what he was looking at. And then I looked at him, and he was already at a stop in the carpool lane, but the bus was coming — it seemed like it was coming so fast, but I don't think it was really fast because we were all at a stop, and all I kept think-ing was he was going to hit the fire truck, and I kept saying, Oh my God, oh my God. And it was — it just hit. It just — it came so fast. I mean, when I think about it, it seems like it was slow motion, but it just came so fast because when I saw him and then looked over at the fire truck and then there was the bus, it just slammed right into the fire truck. And then everything was just moving all over the place, just things flying all over, and I remember the hose — I'm sorry. It's so clear in my mind because I have never seen anything like that be-fore. I remember it hit; it pushed the fire truck but for some reason it came back; it was coming back and everything just went flying all over. I remember seeing the hose because it hit the front of where my car was, and then it just went back toward the other side of the free-way into the slow lanes and hit the side and then faced back the other way. It was — and then we just — I don't remember what I did. It was — everything happened so quickly, and I saw people getting out of their cars so I got out of the car and there were tools all over the place, because I remember seeing this big red tool box to my left. And then when I got out and walked in front where everyone else was, the fireman was already right there on the ground with everyone else. I didn't see them take him out. Everything just happened so quickly.

I saw the Highway Patrol officer talking to several people. He didn't talk to me. Then we were rushed to get off the freeway. And I asked one of the Highway Patrolmen, "Do you want to take a statement?" He said, "No, you need to get off the freeway now." So I turned around and got in my car.

JOHN RUPPERT:

One minute we were slowly making our way to the center divider, the next minute there was a huge jolt and loud explosion. I felt like I was in a clothes dryer, tumbling around with uniforms, boots, turnouts, and wild land gear all around me. Then it stopped, and I sat there in complete silence. Was I knocked out? Did I stay conscious? I did not know. My mind was racing, but my head was moving so slowly, my eyes could not focus. My head throbbed and my hip was shooting with pain, but I was alive. My door was blown wide open and I was looking down a steep hill on the side of the freeway. I looked to my right and saw both doors were also blown wide open, but there was nobody in the driver seat. Where was Tom?

I needed Captain Cascadden. I needed his direction and assurance. I turned around in my seat and saw the back of his head. "Captain Cascadden!" I shouted. Again I yelled "Captain Cascadden!" No reply. I could see his head swaying slowly back and forth and I yelled one more time, "Cascadden!" He turned around to look at me. His eyes were wide open in shock or disbelief. His pupils were fully dilated and he stared straight through me; he was silent. He had blood running down both sides of his face, down his temples, onto his chin. "Are you okay?" I asked. He said nothing. "Are you okay?!" I shouted, and he said "I'm okay." I knew he wasn't. Once again I looked for Tom in the driver's seat and asked Joel, "Where is Tom?" I did not wait for an answer; I went to go see for myself. I climbed down out of the engine and ran around to the other side. I saw Tom on his back a few feet away from the engine; he was not moving, and I thought that Tom was dead.

I had no one to turn to. I was holding Tom's bleeding head in my bare hands; I was scared and I was alone. Tom was alive, but he was barely breathing, gasping for air with a mouthful of blood. I had no medical equipment with me and I was not about to leave Tom to go get it. "Airway," I thought. I had to clear it out and keep him from aspirating blood. I could not turn him over by myself without risking further injury, so I used my fingers to clear the blood, tissue, and broken teeth out of his mouth. I looked up to see a wall of vehicles stopped on the freeway just a few feet from me. It seemed that everybody was out of their cars, standing, staring. A big man, possibly Hawaiian, was slowly approaching me and Tom, looking like he wanted to help. I did not want him touching Tom; I did not trust some stranger with Tom's life. I did know that I needed to get the area around Tom clear so we could work on him, so I yelled at the man and a few others to clear the area. Hose, SCBA, the pump panel, and who knows what else, all spread around like a yard sale on a Saturday morning. A CHP officer came to me and I told him to land an airship on the freeway. He got on the radio and then came to Tom's side to help me.

I needed Captain Cascadden. Last time I saw him, he said "I'm okay," but I knew he wasn't. Joel Cascadden made his way toward Tom and together with the CHP officer we rolled Tom to his side. More blood, clots, tissue, and teeth were cleared out of Tom's mouth. Joel talked to Tom, "Tommy!" he said, "keep breathing." I looked over my right shoulder to see Ontario Fire Medic Engine 135(ME135) hopping over the center divider with their medical equipment. I had help coming, I was no longer alone. Rick Owens, a very experienced paramedic, and his partner showed up shortly after ME135 to assist. Tom was placed in a C-collar, suctioned, and we began assisted ventilations to help him breathe. Tom was moving, he was fighting us, reaching for his neck, so Joel held his arms down while IVs and the intubation kit were being set up. His legs were not moving. Tom was trying to talk; Joel was the first one to hear him. He was mumbling something repetitively. I moved the mask off his face and listened. "I . . . can't . . . breathe," he grunted quietly. "I . . .

can't . . . breathe," he grunted again, gasping for air in between each word. So many things raced through my mind. Hemo/pneumothorax, broken ribs, triple a, torn diaphragm, torn trachea, spinal injury, T-4 maybe? Only one of these I could fix, pneumothorax, but I quickly ruled that out because his lungs were clear and equal. Then I noticed his neck was severely swollen, his throat was pushing up out of the little 2" x 2" square access hole in the front of the cervical collar. I'd never seen that before. I loosened the collar and asked Tom, "Is that better?" "I . . . can't . . . breathe," he said again. I reached in the hole and lifted the collar away from his neck, hoping that would take the pressure off his trachea. "Is that better?" I asked again. "Yes," he said quietly.

Wow, Tom was talking, understanding, helping us help him. I asked Tom where he hurt. He said, "My stomach," as he crossed both hands over his abdomen. With that, Tom was lifted up on the backboard and put onto the ambulance's gurney. The helicopter, Mercy Air, had landed on the freeway, a couple hundred feet from our engine. There must have been seven of us around the gurney, rushing Tom to the chopper. I did not want to be in the way. I've gone on medical aids daily where the family members of the patient either slowed us, or prevented us, from providing the proper care and treatment to the patient. They just want to be part of the solution but end up being part of the problem . . . Was I that guy? I felt, in my mind I was doing everything right, but was I really? I was just in a horrific accident. Joel was hurt bad and Tom might die. My head throbbed and my right leg was shaking. I had been running on pure adrenaline for the last six minutes or so. Was I in the way? At about one hundred feet from the helicopter I let go of the gurney, and stood watching Tom being taken to the helicopter. Within a few seconds, an Ontario fireman grabbed me and said, "Go with him." I ran back to Tom and grabbed his right hand with mine. I saw Rick Owens at the head of the gurney and noticed he had his ball cap on. I asked Rick if his hat would stay on his head. He did not understand me, so I yelled at him, "Take off your hat!" Rick had airlifted *many more patients than I had; he knew what he was doing, and I am sure he knew his hat would stay on. I, however, was not going to take that chance. If anything flew up into that helicopters rotor, it could be grounded, and Tom couldn't afford that. Thankfully Rick threw his hat to the side. I asked Rick to tell Tom to squeeze my hand. Rick leaned in and yelled into Tom's ear; then I felt Tom squeeze my hand as if we were meeting each other for the first time.*

The reports stated that Tom was in the air on his way to Arrowhead Regional Medical Center, the closest trauma center from the scene of the accident, in less than seven minutes from the time of the accident. Joel and I were left in the middle of the freeway.

I began walking back toward the accident, and that was the first time I saw the bus. It was a big, white tour bus, dual axle, up against the center divider with major damage to the front. The freeway was crawling with firemen all wearing yellow, spread out across all lanes. Thousands of feet of bright yellow hose were strewn everywhere. Bus passengers were standing, sitting, and laying down receiving medical treatment. Then I saw our fire engine. It was mangled. I could not believe that a twenty-one ton fire engine could be so severely damaged. It looked as if it had rolled over a few times. I looked around for Joel and noticed he was slowly walking back to the engine; he looked dazed. He was pale and bleeding from his head. An Ontario fireman came up to me and I turned him away, telling him to help my captain as I pointed over toward Joel. He saw me and came toward me; we embraced, but did not say anything. We were both placed on backboards and sent in the same ambulance to Arrowhead. I prayed to God most of the way to the hospital, praying that God would perform a miracle with Tom.

STATEMENT OF THE CHP OFFICER ON THE SCENE OF THE TRAFFIC COLLISION THAT JOEL, TOM, AND JOHN WERE RESPONDING TO THAT MORNING:

Question: *Did you actually see the collision between the bus and the fire engine?*

Answer: *No it was to my left side. The driver of the car was scream-ing like something terrible just happened and at the same time I heard a huge collision or impact. I was standing by the concrete jersey wall in the center divider of the freeway.*

Question: *What did you see?*

Answer: *All I saw at that point was the tour bus coming directly at me. And in my own mind, I thought this bus was going to come run us over. And it was starting to ride up on the K-rail or on the jersey wall to the point where I was thinking this thing was coming over. And it was within eighty feet or so from us when I first observed it. At that point I took as much cover as I could; I ducked and got down low, thinking if this bus came over, we were both dead. I stayed down in that crouched kind of covered position for a couple of brief seconds, and as I was down, I saw the shade of the shroud of the bus go by three feet from me. I mean it was right there. It was going by; I was being showered by pieces of glass and debris and pieces of the bus. I could feel it kind of pelting me in the head and shoulders and then it went on by and I stood up. Immediately after the crash, I radioed Med-Evac for a helicopter.*

Point of impact where the bus hit the fire engine.

Tom was lying almost parallel to the truck with his feet toward the back of the truck in a supine position. The other firefighter came around the back side of the rig and the first thing we did was assist him. We rolled him over so we could assess the airway. The fireman stabilized the head and I opened the airway. At that point he was gurgling out a bunch of blood. He had some major face trauma. No response. He was obviously unconscious. I immediately started suctioning some of the blood out of his airways so he wouldn't drown or aspirate on his own fluids. I suctioned him for two to three minutes and by that time the Ontario Fire Department had arrived. I also used a valve mask as a way of giving him additional ventilations. Tom was breathing, but only a few times a minute. That was not enough to sustain life.

While I was assisting Tom, the fireman was very concerned about his captain. So I went to check on him. I ran to the front of the rig, and the whole front was shattered and the glass was broken out, and I could see him up in the right seat. So I jumped up on the front bumper of the truck and contacted Captain Cascadden through the open front windshield. He had lots of facial cuts. I asked him, "Are you

The fire engine was hit in the fast lane and ended up on the other side of the freeway in pieces.

okay?" I remember him trying to talk on the radio, trying to advise his dispatch what happened. I remember telling him, "Look, if you can come out and help us we could use the help, just come on out," and he did.

I immediately went back to Tom. Captain Cascadden came over to where Tom was and he was at his feet talking to Tom. He kept calling out to him, "Stay with us, Tom. Come on Tom."

After Tom was airlifted to the hospital, I pretty much resumed my original crash site. By that time enough people were there to help out with the triage and all of the folks on the bus.

One of the eyewitness statements that never made it into the final accident report was from the original traffic collision that the fire engine was responding to that morning. The eyewitness was interviewed by the same CHP officer who helped save Tom's life. He was questioned about the interview in his statement.

FURTHER TESTIMONY FROM THE CHP OFFICER:
Question: *Did the witness tell you when you interviewed her that she was stopped in the center divider area waiting for a CHP officer to contact her?*

It is a miracle Joel could climb out of the front window.

Answer: *Yes*

Question: *Did the witness tell you that she saw the fire truck on the eastbound side of the freeway coming across the traffic lanes toward the center divider?*

Answer: *Yes*

Question: *Did the witness say that she saw all of the emergency lights operating on the fire truck.*

Answer: *Yes*

Question: *Did the witness tell you that she saw the other traffic in the eastbound lanes letting the fire truck over toward the left, and that she saw the fire truck continue to come over in the No. 1 lane when she saw the tour bus coming in the carpool lane very fast, possibly seventy-five to eighty miles per hour?*

Answer: *Yes*

Question: *Did the witness tell you that she saw the tour bus approach the fire truck from the rear as the fire truck came over into the carpool lane and that she saw the impact between the tour bus and the fire truck?*

Answer: *Yes*

Question: *Did the witness tell you that she knew something was going to happen because the bus was going too fast?*

Answer: *Yes*

JOEL CASCADDEN:

In March of 2005, Tom and I were on duty at the fire station, just starting our shift. The alarm sounded and we were on our way to another call. "The freeway; I-10, a reported traffic collision." Tom and I talked on the way to the call, not about the call we were responding to, but about the preceding day off, about stuff happening at the station. We didn't talk about the call we were responding to because it was routine, just another freeway response like a hundred times

before. As we entered the freeway, we spotted the accident in the car-
pool lane. "Could we make it over there?" I asked Tom. "Yeah," he
said, and started to make his way across the freeway. Suddenly, there
was an explosion and then darkness turning to light as I was regain-
ing consciousness and looking out through where the windshield once
was. The scene was bizarre, a cop standing in front of the engine
yelling something, my fireman John behind me in the back of the
engine cab yelling something as I tried to make sense of anything I
saw. A gray bus was stopped in the carpool lane across the freeway
and the front was torn off. And Tom was gone. Tom's door was gone,
too. Turning my head over my left shoulder, my eyes met John's. He
was frantic, but once he saw me, he got out. I had to get out, too, first
in slow motion, speeding up to real time. I had to climb out through
the windshield; my door wouldn't open. Walking around the front
of the fire engine, the whole horrible scene unfolded at once. The fire
engine was destroyed, the fire hose spread all across the freeway like
spaghetti and Tom was lying next to the engine in a pool of blood.
Dear God, this was a nightmare. Tom was dead.

The Ontario Fire Department was also instrumental in helping to save
Tom's life. When Ontario Engine 135 arrived on the scene, the captain began ordering additional personnel while the paramedic on the unit tried
to orally intubate Tom. Because he wasn't breathing, he was forced to perform a needle cricothyrotomy, an incision through the skin to secure a patient's airway during certain emergency situations, such as this. A cricotho-
rotomy is usually performed by paramedics as a last resort when control of
the airway by usual means has failed or is not feasible. After inserting the
needle cricothyrotomy, the paramedics continued to bag Tom and again
on the flight to the hospital. I was told this much by the Mercy flight crew
while Tom was in a coma, and it gave me hope that he didn't suffer brain
damage from a lack of oxygen. The emergency personnel performed in absolute harmony that morning to maintain Tom's airway and help save a
fellow firefighter's life. I thank them all for performing flawlessly.

That morning Tom's brother, Paul, who works for the Phoenix Fire
Department, was on a traffic collision call on the 10 freeway in Arizona
at 7:35 a.m. When he returned from the call, he was given the message

that his brother had been in an accident and it didn't look good. The entire Phoenix Fire Department pitched in and made sure that Paul was on a plane and in the waiting room within a few hours. Both brothers were responding to routine traffic collisions that morning, but one of those calls ended in disaster. Paul must have realized his mortality that day as well. Paul spent the next few weeks by Tom's side, returning home intermittently to work and care for his family.

We may never know what actually happened to Tom. The bus hit Tom in the carpool lane and the fire truck ended up on the opposite side of the freeway, yet Tom was found on the freeway twelve feet from the cab door. He didn't have any road rash, indicating that he could not have been thrown from the engine. His front door and seatbelt holder were demolished and he had a significant bruise on his left shoulder, which indicated he had his seatbelt on at the time of the accident. There was an ongoing debate as to whether or not he had his seatbelt on, but no one can convince me otherwise. Joel stated he had it on when he left the station; Tom always wore his seatbelt, and the seatbelt was halfway retracted when the holder was crushed. The only explanation is that it was a faulty latch and upon impact it released and was stuck partially retracted when the bus hit the back of the fire engine. This explained the seatbelt, but his final loca-

1" tubular steel bent by Tom's body during the accident.

tion continues to be a mystery. Did he get thrown from the fire engine or did he get out of the fire truck and pass out after walking a few feet? No one really knows because no one actually witnessed what happened.

Later that summer Tom's best friend from high school, Dan Shier, came to visit us with his family. As we were all discussing the accident, Dan kept asking how he ended up in that position on the freeway. Tom and I both said we couldn't explain it. Dan's wife offered the first explanation that seemed possible in my mind. She said, "Perhaps angels lifted him out of the fire engine and gently placed him on the ground." After all of the miracles we received surrounding Tom's injuries, I would have to be foolish not to consider it as an option.

Chapter 5: *Breaking All the Rules*

I do not set aside the grace of God, for if righteousness
could be gained through the law, Christ died for nothing.
GALATIANS 2:21

I WAS SO SCARED WHEN TOM WAS IN THE HOSPITAL. I KNEW THE dangers of being in hospitals long term and the longer he was there the more likely he would contract an infection. I was even reminded that if I didn't leave the hospital at least once a day and get some fresh air, I would most likely get sick. At this point I wished I was completely ignorant. I sat in the county hospital knowing that every procedure would expose Tom to risks. Most intensive care units (ICU) have very strict policies prohibiting family members from visiting outside of regular visiting hours. I didn't have to ask for permission. No one left Tom's side, not for a moment. Tom even had friends with him in the helicopter ride from the freeway to the hospital. The nurse on the helicopter was friends with Tom's brother, Mike. The extended family of firefighters is larger than I could have ever comprehended.

Tom's accident was on a Tuesday morning. He was admitted to his room in the ICU that afternoon. From the time he was admitted into his room until the day he was released from the rehabilitation hospital, he had an advocate by his side every second of the day. For the first three days I only left the hospital to be with our two daughters. They needed to hear what happened from me. I left that afternoon to tell Rebecca, age ten and Catie, age seven, that their father had been in a bad accident and mommy needed to be with their daddy. I knew they needed to hear it from me and I needed to see them. I needed to hug them, to know that they were all right. The bus seemed to hit my entire life that day and it felt as though it were the end of my world.

Seeing Catie and Rebecca gave me hope. I was counseled by the nurses and psychologists that it probably wasn't a good idea to let Rebecca and

Catie see their father. If he were to die, they would always remember him distorted and not like the man he was. This thought was traumatic enough, what did I know. Perhaps they were right. If the sight of Tom made grown men cry, how could I expose our children to such trauma? I opted to wait to let the girls see Tom. He had tubes coming from every part of his body, a tracheotomy, three chest tubes, a tube coming out of his head checking his inter-cranial pressure, a catheter, IVs and monitors where there was exposed skin. I mentally decided to wait until the tube in his head was removed. At that point I would let the girls visit their father. Until then, I would visit them daily, give them updates, and record their voices for Tom to hear. I would use a tape recorder to let the girls talk to Tom and then play it back for Tom in the ICU. Catie was more responsive and assured her father that everyone was praying for him, even people in Alaska. I don't know where that came from, but it was important to her that Tom knew that. Rebecca was more reserved and just wanted her father to know that she missed him and loved him. When I played the tape recorder for Tom, I think it made the nurses realize that this just wasn't another patient but a father to two young daughters. I asked Catie and Rebecca not only to draw pictures for Tom, but to write thank you letters to the hospital staff for taking such good care of their father.

For the first three days after the accident Tom was completely unconscious, yet he was asked to respond to hourly neuro-checks with a thumbs up. I understood the reasons for these routine procedures, but found them torturous. My mind would wander and think Tom didn't respond to that last request, he wouldn't open his eyes, he wouldn't motion his thumb. His brain was dead, wasn't it? God, why wasn't he responding?

In addition to the hourly neuro-checks, the nurses would check his blood sugar via a finger stick. Apparently doctors found better results in brain injury patients if their blood sugar was maintained at a certain level. I believe that Tom knew he had someone by his side every moment. Later I asked Tom how he felt when he was in his coma. He told me it was like an emptiness, all black, nothing there. I wondered if he saw angels or if God was talking to him. When he told me it was all black, I was so discouraged. I wondered if Tom really knew God. Would Tom be in heaven if he died? Is there a heaven? Tom had been raised Catholic and I always assumed he knew Jesus and would go to heaven. While Tom was in his coma, I read him the Bible so he would be comforted. I wanted him to hear those words that sustained my sanity. There were times I felt the presence of God in the room so intensely that it seemed as though His arms were holding me up. How could Tom have missed this amazing experience? God must have been working on another part of Tom's body and knew that I was the one who needed the mental comfort.

After his surgeries, Tom was brought back up to the ICU and his family and friends were given a private waiting room inside the ICU. I am sure the administrators at the hospital broke all of their rules that day, but perhaps the incredible recovery of Tom will make them rethink some of their policies.

People were allowed to see Tom one at a time and were asked to be quiet and keep the visit short. I will never forget the look on fellow firefighters' faces as they went in the room to visit Tom. The tears that fell from their eye and the looks of sorrow made me wonder what they were thinking. I saw the same look in hundreds of fellow firefighters. I later realized that Tom represented each one of them. Tom was the statistic waiting to happen and they were seeing it right in front of their own eyes. They were able to see the consequences of the violence and dangers of their profession.

Tom had gone on a call on the freeway and he became the victim of a careless bus driver trying to get to a casino. How many other careless bus drivers are there in this world? People are driving while on their cell phones and so self-absorbed they don't even slow down for an emergency vehicle. The firefighters and paramedics see it every day. How many near misses had they had in their careers? Today the near miss became a reality. Tom was driving 10 mph on the freeway that morning, yet he was so violently hit by a bus traveling 78 mph that his entire body was bruised, his face was swollen, his eyes looked like charcoal, his teeth were missing, his lungs collapsed, and he was left looking like a monster. It was a sight so tragic and disturbing that I know it must have been difficult for his fellow firefighters, friends, and family to see and probably made them question their own mortality. Yet I know their presence in the room gave Tom strength and gave him the energy to fight for his life. They openly prayed for his healing. They were there twenty-four hours a day, seven days a week. Their dedication to their brother blessed me. They were angels in disguise. Every single one of them.

What if the hospital administrators had forbidden those visits? In the many years that I have worked in hospitals I have always questioned the traditional medical model of caring for patients. I have a deep appreciation for the advancements in medical technology, but in recent years have grown to question the point of diminishing return. Have we forgotten the power of social support and prayer? The body is not only a physical being, but an emotional and spiritual one as well. I know there are many health professionals who are asking the same questions. There is a balance between medical technology and complementary medicine. Tom is a perfect case study in which this was shown to be successful. The extremely capable emergency medical system allowed Tom to stay alive long enough for the power of social support and prayer to take effect. Even if Tom hadn't survived, shouldn't he have been surrounded by his family and friends? Perhaps initially that is why he was allowed so many visits. I know the hospital staff did not believe Tom would survive. Maybe they were being humane. I may never know, but I do know I am grateful for the few restrictions placed on the visitations to Tom.

There was a delicate balance between visitation for Tom and not over stimulating him. He was in critical condition and the doctors needed him to be calm. All the visitors were so respectful about limiting themselves to two-at-a-time, staying quiet, and limiting the time. The nurses were sure to put a note on Tom's door, "Please be quiet, I am tired and I need my rest." It was as if the note was from Tom. Everyone respected these ground rules for Tom as well as for the other patients in the hospital. I remember many of Tom's visitors consoling other family members. The ICU in a county hospital can be a very sad place. I would like to believe that many of the angels that visited Tom touched the lives of the other patients as well.

Hospital rooms are so sterile and miserable. Not that I would encourage increasing the cost of health care with expensive decorations in hospital rooms, but why can't hospital rooms be designed to be more humane? Intensive care units are filled with trauma, misery, and sadness. Little touches in the environment could make a world of difference for patients who open their eyes for the first time after being in a coma. My sister, Kelly, works for a neurologist and recommended that I put up pictures of Tom in his room. It reminded the nursing staff that this patient was not the disfigured patient he appeared to be, but a father, a son, a husband,

A shrine was created by fellow firefighters in Tom's hospital room.

a brother, and a friend. Again the hospital staff was accommodating to allow pictures of family, drawings from nieces and nephews, and even a shrine to the fire department put up by fellow firefighters. I returned one day to find Tom's helmet, shirt, badge, and award for being firefighter of the year placed alongside the American flag and sign from the demolished fire engine. The sight took my breath away.

As the days progressed and the news stories inhabited every local station and newspaper, cards from students came pouring in until Tom's room was covered in cards from local schools. It was almost as if the community was wrapping its arms around Tom with the love being written on every wall of his hospital room. There was one note from a third-grade student that I will never forget:

"Fireman Barilla,
Thank you for reading Stellaluna to our class. I am sorry you were hurt and I hope you feel better soon."

Stellaluna is one of my favorite children's books, a touching story that I read to my children often. I wondered if Tom read that book to the children upon their request or because he knew it was one of my favorites. Regardless, the note from this elementary school child brought a smile to my face when I had very little to smile about. People often do not realize the power of a simple gesture.

Tom had given to his community for fifteen years and they gave back in his hour of need. The law of reciprocity does work. Tom was determined to get back to work to give back to his community. I believe the power of community support was as important a component as his medical care during his rehabilitation.

Tom loved music. He played it all the time and told me it was his escape. I thought he might enjoy hearing music despite his unconscious state. I brought in his favorite CDs and played them day and night. I would picture him singing his favorite song and talk about the times that coincided with the songs. I later asked Tom if he remembered hearing the music. He said no, but thanked me for playing it. He thought that was a great idea.

Even the music couldn't take away the unforgettable smell of Tom's hospital room. It was the smell of death. The medicines, the bodily fluids, and the antiseptics all made a combination that was nauseating. I was determined to try and clean Tom. If I could only get rid of the smell of death. I spent hours washing the parts of his body that were visible and cleaning the remnants of blood from his ears, head, and mouth. It wasn't as if he wasn't being well cared for, but I wanted him to be clean. I cannot explain why I felt this way, but for some strange reason, it was important to me. On top of his daily cleaning, I spent hours massaging his feet and other parts of his body that were visible. I would use lotion from a gift basket to rub his feet at least four times a day. Everyone was focusing on his inter-cranial pressure, his oxygen levels, his respiration, and blood sugar. I needed another focus. I couldn't take another neuro-check. I would provide Tom with what the medical model had long forgotten, a lot of tender loving care.

For the first week after Tom's accident, I stayed the night with Tom as much as possible, trading shifts with other fellow firefighters who let me sleep for an hour or two in the waiting room. It was often the late-night discussions that were times of stillness and peace for me. Every night and every morning I was sure to run into someone cleaning Tom's room who let me know they were praying. They told me that Tom's brother asked them to pray and they wanted me to know that they were praying. The response to this request is the miracle that saved Tom's life. People prayed and they let me know they were praying. One morning I walked into the waiting room and there was a balloon, a stuffed animal, and a card signed by the entire Environmental Services Department sending us love and prayers. It was as if they were my contact with the outside world and they were sending me messages that the world was praying. Even an older gentleman cleaning the hallways during a midnight walk told me that the doctors didn't always know the outcome and that our God was a powerful God and that He could heal those in need. "Ma'am, I am praying for your husband."

I am sure those working graveyard cleaning intensive care units at county facilities witness an incredible amount of trauma and sorrow. I am sure most hospitals would have fired their staff for what they did. I thank God every day that this staff was given the freedom to express themselves. The kind words of the environmental services department at the Arrowhead Regional Medical Center touched me in ways I will never forget; they impacted my life in profound and meaningful ways.

Every day following the accident food would be delivered starting at noon for all the family and friends visiting Tom. I often wondered how this was orchestrated, but like clockwork some local fire department would deliver food for about twenty or thirty people for both lunch and dinner. Every morning coffee was made by five a.m. from the daily delivery of fresh Starbucks, and the pot brewed until late in the evening. Local restaurants provided complimentary meals and local police and fire departments would pick them up and deliver them. I wasn't very hungry at the time, but I remember thinking about the kindness of these gestures.

Inevitably food would be left over, so we would offer the hospital staff a late night snack. We were sure to take good care of our nursing staff. I knew there were limits to gifts staff could receive from patients and their families, but the gifts were from so many people and the rules and procedures seemed irrelevant. This is what it is like to take care of your own. I had heard about this in religious communities, but I had never witnessed it for myself. I have been involved in church communities most of my life and never had I seen a church take care of its own members the way the firefighters took care of my family.

For the first three days after Tom's accident, most of the firefighters were at the hospital. I finally asked one of the men who was covering calls for the city of Upland. The explanation could not be possible. Tom's accident had been so widely publicized on television that other departments came to cover the Upland stations so the Upland fire department could be together as a family. Engines as far as Pasadena (about thirty-five miles west of Upland) sent engines to cover the city. Often surrounding cities will cover in times of emergencies, but rarely did you see engines that far away covering calls. Firefighters who had long-been retired came back and offered to help. We have pictures of the Pasadena Fire Department putting out a fire in the parking lot of Upland City Hall. Friends now laugh at the picture and remember that time fondly, not because Tom was in critical condition, but because it felt good to do the right thing.

An extended family came to help in those seventy-two hours that Tom was in critical condition. Potential litigation and rigid policies would have prohibited this in the past. Thankfully, that day the interim fire chief was a man who cared more about people than policies and had the courage to do the right thing. The fire chief had the courage to help his firefighters cope with a terrible tragedy by displaying the best of humanity.

Chapter 6: *Community Support*

Though you have made me see troubles, many and bitter,
you will restore my life again; from the depths of the earth
you will again bring me up. You will increase my honor
and comfort me once again.
PSALM 71:20-21

OM ALWAYS USED TO SAY THAT AIR CONDITIONING AND GARAGE door openers were the downfall of society. He complained that we don't talk to our neighbors. We come home, close our garages, and live our lives inside of our houses. Tom would have been so proud of his community had he been conscious to how how they came together on March 15, 2005.

I am so grateful today for the support we received from our community. I believe that a major part of Tom's recovery was because of that community support. The Bible clearly states that "Faith without works is dead." (James 2:20) People not only prayed, they gave of their time, their talents, and their money without ever being asked.

The hospital was constantly filled with people sending food, magazines, lip balm, and blankets. I was told that after we left, the hospital staff expressed how much they missed us. They were blessed to see the acts of kindness being expressed to Tom.

So often in times of tragedy, people don't know what to do for the family. Let me assure you that simple acts of kindness are more powerful than you could ever imagine. I had one friend who sent me cards of encouragement throughout Tom's recovery. Those cards were often sitting in the mailbox at the end of a long day of rehabilitation and carried me through the next day. Lisa Griffin, a wife of a fellow firefighter, had a gift for sharing inspirational thoughts just when I needed them most. Often they included passages from the Bible of encouragement. God's word is so powerful. I felt as though I was in this constant battle to feel sorry for myself. Why, God, was this happening? But because of the community support I received, I couldn't stay in my pity party for long. How could I feel sorry for myself when I was really so blessed?

The day of Tom's accident a fellow firefighter went to get Subway sandwiches for everyone in the waiting room. It was late at night and no one had eaten for hours. The firefighter had an Upland uniform on when he went into the sandwich shop next to the hospital. He ordered several dozen sandwiches and went to pay when he realized that they were already paid for. The customer in front of the firefighter noticed the Upland uniform and knew why he was buying the sandwiches and paid for them anonymously. Even the firefighter was touched by the generosity of a stranger in a sandwich shop.

One day I came home from Casa Colina, where Tom had been moved for rehab, and found a card on my doorstep from one of my dear friends Shirley Simmons. She had sent a check, along with a card of encouragement, telling me to take the money and get a pedicure. She knew this was one of those simple pleasures I enjoyed. So the next day after dropping Tom off, I drove to the Claremont Club just up the street from Casa Colina and asked if they had any openings for a pedicure. Luckily, a lovely young girl by the name of Robin was available. As I sat in the massage chair, I began to share that my husband had been in an accident and I hadn't had much time to do anything, let alone paint my nails, and asked her to forgive the pathetic condition of my toes. To my pleasant surprise, Robin asked me about Tom's injury. I was shocked at her intimate knowledge of what I was experiencing. What could this young girl know about the trauma of a severe brain injury? Apparently she knew far more than I did. It was only a few years prior that her husband had been in a coma for four months from a skiing accident. Furthermore, he was airlifted to Arrowhead Regional Medical Center and been at Casa Colina for months following his brain injury. Her story gave me chills down my spine. What were the odds of me meeting this woman? Robin and I talked for hours and she brought me so much comfort. Her husband was now back at work and functioning very well. Later that week I received a card from Robin encouraging me and offering a free pedicure and manicure for both of my daughters. Shirley's kindness had an exponential effect that day. Meeting Robin was a gift and I consider her to be one of the angels that got me through my next round of challenges. She was such a blessing.

I continued to spend hours at the hospital for several weeks. This was an incredible strain on my family. My children needed me and by the time I came home at the end of the day I was physically and mentally exhausted. Life continued to move on, although it felt as though I was stuck in a bubble and I couldn't move on with the rest of the world.

I was driving back and forth from home to the hospital and to the children's school. One day as I was in the line of cars waiting to pick up the girls at school, the mother of one of Catie's friends said she had been trying to find me, because she had a basket she wanted to share with me. She got out of her car and brought it to me. I thanked her and continued in the line of cars to pick up the girls. Sitting in my car and waiting, I began to look inside the basket. Again, I was completely overwhelmed. The entire school had donated money and purchased gift cards for our family. The gift cards were for gas and food. The basket was full. How could anyone be that kind? I didn't pay for gas or make dinner for a month. I was able to focus all of my energy on Tom and the girls. Tom continued to progress and the girls blossomed as we began to heal as a family. Those gift cards showed the girls that they were supported and loved by their school. School was a safe and supportive environment. Their teachers helped carry my children during that time period, taking extra effort to make sure they were adjusting. No, my children did not attend private school. This was our public school in our local community. Thank you. I am confident that my children will be forever moved by the incredible kindness the community showed to them in their time of tragedy.

I don't know how to give back all that I have been given. I couldn't buy enough thank-you cards and don't know half the people who helped us. The love of our community was a significant part of our healing journey. Those simple kind gestures carried me on the days I couldn't get off the bathroom floor. It prevented me from falling into the black hole of self pity. I thank God for all those simple kind gestures. My hope is that those who read this book will know how powerful small gestures can be to someone experiencing a tragedy. You don't need to be philosophical or say the right thing to someone in pain; sometimes just a card, a cooked meal, a smile, or just being there and holding someone in your arms, saying nothing at all is enough.

I was given a gift of enormous community support that I had no idea existed. I believe God sent His army to support me because I cried out for help. But I am not unique. What God gave me, he would give to anyone who asked. If you are experiencing a tragedy, don't be afraid to ask for help. God's promises are available for us all. If you are reading this because you know someone who is experiencing a tragedy, don't underestimate the small acts of kindness. Often it was the cup of coffee or a simple smile that revealed Jesus to me most.

Chapter 7: *The Firefighter Family*

THE SUPPORT I RECEIVED FROM THE FIREFIGHTERS WAS SO AMAZING it deserved its own chapter. They were a key component of the community support that our family received. At one point I felt guilty about all of the help I was receiving and tried to refuse help when one day a firefighter kindly reminded me that they weren't only doing it for Tom and our family. He said that when they were helping us out, they were also showing their own families that they would be taken care of if any of them were lying injured in the bed. "Now my wife knows she will be okay if something happens to me."

JOEL CASCADDEN:
Twenty-nine years I've been riding in fire engines. As a fire captain, I command fire crews at emergency scenes varying from broken arms, heart attacks, traffic collisions, and of course, fires. Firefighters have a special bond because of the work we do and the environment we work in. In essence, we become family, a brotherhood. With any family there are members you like more than others and some you become very close to. Tom, my engineer, is like that. He is not only my co-worker; he is my friend.

The definition of community is a social group of any size whose members reside in a specific locality, share government, and often have a common cultural and historical heritage. Firefighters are the most beautiful loving community I have ever experienced in my life. If you ever doubted the power of social support in healing, I would ask you to seriously reconsider. From the moment Tom was hit by the bus, his fellow firefighters came to his rescue. Firefighter John Rupert immediately came to Tom's rescue; he was a probationary fireman who became the commander on the freeway that morning. He found Tom on the freeway covered in blood, and didn't hesitate; he took care of Tom and made sure others took care of Joel. Moments later a fellow firefighter-paramedic from the neighboring city arrived on scene and started working on Tom. He performed a drastic procedure that was instrumental in saving Tom's life and prevented further brain damage. The heroism and dedication of those two firefighters was only the beginning of the support we would receive.

From the moment Lou Steslicki, an Upland division chief, opened the emergency room doors and escorted me in to see Tom, a firefighter never left my side. Regardless of what room I was whisked off to, a firefighter was with me. After a week at the hospital, I went to use the restroom and realized I did not know how to open the door in the ICU. There had been someone there to meet my every need. It was at that point I realized how blessed I truly had been. Regardless of my need, a firefighter or spouse was there for me. I was driven to and from the hospital when I visited my children, my children were cared for, my house was cleaned, my lawns were mowed, my bills were paid, my pool was cleaned, and I never had to ask. I thank God for that support. I am not one to ask for help and I needed it desperately. I am so grateful I never had to ask.

One of my favorite stories is from an Upland firefighter who was in Alaska at the Iditarod at the time of the accident. A local happened to have a remote TV in one of the towns and they were watching CNN. The news story had run several times on national media. He realized it was his department and one of his was in danger and he needed to get home. All of the locals helped him to catch a plane that was held up on the runway so he could board and make it home to his fallen friend. He travelled for about twenty hours, but when he arrived in Los Angeles, he went directly to the hospital and sat in the waiting room.

On March 29, 2005, my daughter Rebecca received a notice that she would be getting an award at school with an invitation for her parents to attend. I can't explain why, but when I read the letter I broke down in tears at the hospital. It occurred to me that I might be the only one attending awards ceremonies in the near future. One of the captains noticed I was crying while reading my mail and asked me what was wrong. I mentioned the awards ceremony and he said he would take care of it. I wasn't sure what that meant, but I found out the morning of the awards ceremony. An engine along with four uniformed firefighters showed up at the school to take the place of their fallen co-worker. In addition, four off-duty firemen showed up to watch Rebecca receive her award. We sat in the front row that morning. When Rebecca's teacher called her up, she publicly made an announcement about Tom's accident and asked the school for their thoughts and prayers. I cannot begin to tell you how special I felt that day. Chivalry is not dead. I have never been one to need to be saved but that day I felt like a queen and so did my daughter.

REBECCA BARILLA:
I was so sad my dad couldn't be there, but the fact that all of those people took the time to come to my honor roll assembly made it the best assembly ever. I felt so special. I was sad, but so touched, that people really cared about me. My teacher mentioned my dad's accident and I thought "people care." That meant a lot.

The fire department held fundraisers for our family. The generosity of the community completely overwhelmed me. The most touching donation was $100 given by a low-income senior apartment complex in Upland. The seniors had pooled their money and sent $100 and a note thanking Tom for his service to the city. Tears still come to my eyes when I think of the love and support behind that donation. It continues to motivate me to give back what I have been given. Those seniors motivate me to make my community a better place.

After several weeks at Arrowhead Regional Medical Center Tom began his rehabilitation at Casa Colina in Pomona. Directly across the street from the hospital was the local fire department. Tom had attended paramedic school in 2003 and performed his internship in Pomona with the local fire department. We were visited in the hospital *every* day by a crew in Pomona asking if we needed anything and giving me their number to call 24/7. Although I didn't really need anything and never called, knowing I had that support brought me so much peace.

Tom told me that he had a pact with his brother Mike. They promised each other that if either of them were hurt, the other one would take care of their family. Tom can rest assured that his brother was faithful to his pact. Mike never left my side. He was there for me every step of the way. I know that Mike was hurting so badly during Tom's recovery, but he was always the pillar of strength. Late one night at Arrowhead Regional Medical Center Tom was still in a coma, but we had finally been given hope that he was going to live. Mike broke down and cried and said, "Dore, he is going to live." (Mike always called me Dore instead of Dora.) I didn't realize that Mike never had a chance to grieve. He was too busy taking care of me, my family, and Tom.

Mike was also supported by the firefighters in his own department for the city of Pasadena. Their department donated time to give Mike a month off to be with his brother. Immediately following the accident, the Pasadena Fire Department brought so much food to Mike and his family that they ran out of room in their refrigerator. This did not stop their kindness. The next day they showed up with a new refrigerator and diligently stocked it with food for over a month. The kindness and compassion exhibited by their deeds restored my faith in mankind. The true miracle is that people exhibited such thoughtfulness.

Joel, Tom's captain, was also there for me and my family throughout the ordeal. Although Joel had broken several of his ribs during the accident, he refused to leave Tom's side at the hospital. We finally had to force him to go home that first night because there was nowhere to sit in the waiting room. He left for a few hours of rest that evening and was back the next day, never to leave our side. Joel called me every day and visited anytime I needed anything. He slept in the hospital with Tom, gave me his shoulder to cry on, protected me from the media, advocated for Tom at every step, and walked through the litigation with us.

Local fire departments volunteered their time and resources to cover all of the calls so Tom's fellow firefighters could be with him. The coverage did not stop at surrounding cities; retired firefighters volunteered to come in and help out, cities hours away offered their coverage, and even drove engines out to Upland to show their support for their fallen brother.

During the first week of Tom's accident, a crew from the Upland Fire Department mowed our lawns with a schedule to continue until Tom could do it himself. My neighbors brought food for my children, my children's teachers stopped by, flowers filled my living room, blood donations filled the local blood bank, and baskets from neighboring fire departments with movies, toys, and gift certificates were there constantly for my children.

Several weeks after the accident I received a note from Los Angeles County Fire Department that read "If you need any assistance that Upland Fire, family, or friends cannot provide in a timely manner, please call on one of us. We will be there to assist in any way possible. Take care . . . Troy." This note, along with a list of names and home phone numbers, was left for me at Casa Colina.

The support from the firefighter family transcended generations. The son of a firefighter who had worked withTom years ago at Sierra Madre Fire Department was attending La Salle High School in Pasadena, the same high school Tom attended in the 1980s. He put together a fundraiser for our family. He asked his fellow students to pay one dollar and in return, the students would not have to wear their school uniform on a designated day to honor Tom. The school raised $1,200. The money meant far less to me than the thoughtfulness of a teenage boy who cared enough to go out of his way to help someone in need. It also revealed to me that this young man's father had modeled compassion and sacrifice for others that was so widespread in the fire service.

Firefighters take care of their own. No one can ever deny this fact. We wouldn't need government programs if the world was more like the fire service. When people are down on their luck, fellow citizens lend a helping hand to their fellow men. What a simple concept that could, in fact, change the world we live in.

It is true what Aesop said: "No act of kindness, no matter how small, is ever wasted." I remember every kind gesture. Several months after the accident I realized I hadn't picked up my dry cleaning. When I walked into the dry cleaners, I gave my name to the lady working behind the counter and asked her for the balance. She asked if my husband was the firefighter in "that" accident. I nodded my head and said yes. She said someone came in one day and saw my name and paid for my dry cleaning. I broke down in tears, along with the lady behind the counter and the other customers. Even months after the publicity, people were still offering their kindness. Several months later, I found out the good samaritan was the Ontario fire captain on the scene of the accident that morning. Again, a simple gesture by a fellow firefighter touched everyone in the cleaners that day.

I could not comprehend the kindness. I have tried to avoid asking why this horrible tragedy happened, but I can say that if it had to happen I could not have been more blessed with love and support surrounding me every second. The generosity exhibited during Tom's accident made giving contagious. It blessed so many people I felt God by me every second of this tragedy. I was carried by God's angels in disguise, the firefighters.

Chapter 8: *Faith —*
Holding on During the Storm

My grace is sufficient for you, for my
power is made perfect in weakness.
2 CORINTHIANS 12:9

DAILY BULLETIN
RECOVERY "A MIRACLE" FOR FIREFIGHTER
FIREFIGHTER'S WIFE CREDITS FAITH FOR HIS SURVIVAL
(Original pub. date: 3/27/2005)
Edward Barrera, Staff Writer
Article Launched: 04/05/2006 11:45:00 PM PDT

*UPLAND — Surrounded by walls covered with get-well cards in
an Arrowhead Regional Center waiting room, Dora Barilla recalls
being told the news of her husband's condition after a freeway crash
March 15.*

*An Upland firefighter, Tom Barilla suffered major head and
chest injuries in a collision on the 10 Freeway as he and two other
firefighters were responding to an emergency call. Despite knowing
that the forty-year-old firefighter was battling for survival, Dora Barilla said she never doubted he would pull through.*

*"It is a miracle that he is alive," Barilla said on Saturday, adding
later, "But I believe in miracles."*

*Sitting with family and friends, Dora Barilla described the 2004
Upland Firefighter of the Year as having a dynamic personality and
being full of humor. But he was also committed to helping others.*

"We both have a sense of service," she said. "We share that, and you don't question that. You do what you are called to do."

Barilla said she expected Tom's steady recovery because of her religious faith and because she knew he was a battler. But she wasn't expecting the outpouring of assistance from firefighters throughout the area.

"I was overwhelmed," the thirty-five-year-old health-care consultant said. "If the world was more like the fire service, this would be a much better place."

The help included local firefighters manning Upland fire stations so that Barilla's colleagues could visit, bring daily deliveries of home-cooked food, or even simpler gestures.

"I was here for five straight days, and I don't ever remember opening the door," she said, smiling.

Mike Barilla, Tom's brother and a Pasadena firefighter, said while it's common for fellow firefighters to help in times of crisis, even he was taken aback by the reaction.

"I know there is somewhat of a fine line, each department usually takes care of its own," he said. "But with this event, the line never existed."

The Barilla family and friends said they know Tom has a rough road ahead. Friday was the first day his two daughters, Rebecca, 10, and Catie, 7, saw their father.

After several surgeries, with another expected in several months, Tom is able to recognize people and respond with hand signals. He still has a trachea tube to help with breathing, and arduous rehabilitation begins in several weeks.

But Barilla's neurologist, Dr. Javed Siddiqi, said if Barilla's steady progress continues, he could make a good recovery within six to twelve months.

It's that optimism that Dora Barilla, who quit her job to take care of Tom, said she is counting on.

"I'm standing on the fact that God is going to complete his miracle," she said.

I CALLED MY FRIEND RENEE AND ASKED HER TO PUT TOM ON THE prayer chain of my church the morning of the accident. I didn't have the details, but I knew people needed people to pray. Along with calls of other fellow believers who had heard about the accident, this was the beginning of Tom's healing.

Since the night that I fell to my knees at the side of my bed and God gave me those words of comfort, "Dora, stop asking me to heal Tom and start praising me for healing Tom," I had a peace that sustained me even through the most challenging moments.

A brain injury does not only affect the injured individual, but the entire family and circle of friends, also. It turns your life upside down and inside out, as though you are spinning on the axis of this earth in isolation. Everything else is moving forward and you are stuck in this pocket of life that won't move. It is almost as if the oxygen in your pocket isn't sufficient and you wonder if you are going to suffocate. A brain injury is like the perfect storm that hits your life and you wonder if you will survive, and I am not referring to the patient, but the family. I often tease Tom and tell him that he had the easy part; after all, he has no recollection of the accident, the surgeries, the coma, the intensive care unit, and minimal recollection of rehabilitation. The family, on the other hand, lived the nightmare, which will never be removed from their memory.

When I was told that Tom's chances of survival were minimal, I remember the absolute emptiness that I initially felt, as if a meteor landed in the middle of my existence. I sat and listened to the doctors tell me the prognosis, "We are going to have to remove his skull," and truly felt the definition of surreal. At the time, it didn't occur to me that the doctors could put the skull back and I wondered how someone could live without part of his skull. This was the first of multiple surgeries and obstacles Tom faced.

A good friend, Larry Enriquez, who is also a pastor, came to visit me several times at Arrowhead Regional Medical Center. He would pray with me while Tom was still in a coma and was cognizant that I was putting on quite a front to get through the day. He used to say to me, "Dora, I know it is Friday and that things seem dark and painful, but let me guarantee you that Sunday is coming." I held onto those words and believed that my life was a living hell at the moment, but God's glory was just around the corner.

During the surgeries, the waiting rooms were full of people I hadn't seen in years. Should I talk to them in my comatose state? After all, shouldn't I be hospitable? I didn't think I had the strength . . .

Cheri Weaver, the wife of Tom's best friend, sat at my feet comforting me during Tom's first surgery. I remember my eyes were so swollen I had a difficult time seeing, but as she held my hand I noticed a word on her ring; it said JESUS. I said, "Jesus is going to heal Tom, right?" She took off her ring and put it on my right hand and said yes. That ring meant so much to me. Every time I would feel as though that meteor was going to destroy me, I would look at my hand and be reminded of God's gift to us, Jesus.

As people began to fill the waiting rooms and the press began to gather at the hospital and my energy became almost minimal, I looked at my ring and God said, "Ask these people to pray." What if God's people prayed? What if I really believed God could heal Tom? Do we ask and not believe? I made a conscious decision to get on my knees and pray until they pronounced Tom dead. I was going to pray for his complete healing. I asked the firemen in the room to pray for Tom; it was a beautiful sight to see the firemen in the room all hold hands and pray aloud for Tom. The picture of those firefighters in uniform praying in the waiting room to this day brings me such a sense of peace.

Unfortunately my pastor was out of town during Tom's accident, but we were blessed to have our assistant pastor and his wife, Terry and Vicki Herman, comfort us in the waiting room that day.

Several days after Tom's accident, Vicki gave me a bracelet with hanging angels. I love angels. She said that the bracelet was a reminder of God's faithfulness for several other tragedies and she wanted me to have it. She stated that after each tragedy, an angel mysteriously disappeared and there were only three angels left. I wore that bracelet every day and as predicted, lost an angel. Several months later, I found the broken angel on the floor by my bed. I still keep the angel next to my bed as a reminder of the faith that I had during Tom's accident and that if God was faithful then, He will be faithful again. His love and power are right there if I would only believe.

PASTOR STEVE DEYOUNG'S (TOM & DORA'S PASTOR):
While on vacation, I received the news that Tom had been in a horrific accident and he might not survive. I did what most people would do, I began to pray. I prayed that God would give the doctors wisdom, the family comfort, and that Tom would somehow pull through.

I got back in town as quickly as I could and met the family at the hospital, not knowing what to expect when I walked through those doors for the first time. What I saw brought tears to my eyes. The waiting room was filled with firemen and others comforting each other, praying, and supporting each other in every way they knew how. I even commented to the firemen how amazing it was to see the brotherhood in action. After all, isn't that what we should do for each other in times like these.

The work of the hands of so many in action, bringing comfort to those in need, was truly remarkable. However, when Dora and I walked into Tom's room and I saw him for the first time, I realized no hands of man could fix Tom. This was going to take the hand of God.

The power of prayer is an amazing thing. As Dora and I stood and prayed, faith welled up in my heart as I realized nothing was impossible with God. And as we all know, Tom is a walking testament to answered prayer. Tom may not have ever wanted to be a miracle, but he is one, and all the glory goes to God.

I was totally stripped of any control the day of Tom's accident; I was forced into total submission to God. I always believed in God, I prayed every day, I read the Bible often, and attended church just about every Sunday, but at that moment I was so thankful for my intimate relationship with God. God was with me; I could feel him carry me. He was my strength.

As these thoughts came to me, I was reminded of the poem, "Footprints in the Sand," by Mary Stevenson. I have always loved the poem, which tells the story of a man who dreamed he walked with the Lord, yet when he looked back on the path of his life, he saw only one set of footprints, leading him to believe the Lord had left him during his most troubling times. As the man learned, the Lord did not desert him; there were only one set of prints because the Lord carried him during those times.

Tom's brother Mike reminded me of that poem late one evening when I was struggling to stay composed. Although I always appreciated the poem, I never felt the author's pain or the motivation for writing that poem until after March 15, 2005. I knew this was the scene in my life that God carried me.

After the press conferences, I began to receive letters confirming that God's people were praying. We had letters from small children, school kids and staff, strangers in other countries, and old friends who heard about Tom through a prayer chain. My aunt in Ohio asked her gardener to pray for her niece's firefighter husband who had been hit by a bus and was hurt badly. He responded that he was already praying for him, because his wife had received a prayer request from their church. I probably will never know all of the people who prayed for Tom but know we are so grateful for their prayers. They are the true heroes! We thank God for their faithfulness.

When Tom returned to work, he was in the grocery store buying food in uniform and the checker noticed his name and said, "You are the one; I prayed for you." Tom smiled and said thank you; "It worked." This occurrence happened in different scenarios time and time again. Now when I receive a prayer request I don't take it lightly. Somewhere, someone I don't know might be going through a terrible storm, needing God's people to pray. I constantly ask myself if I have made the time in my life to be available to others. I think we have become so busy in our daily lives really getting nothing accomplished because we forgot to take time to pray.

God revealed himself to me in a way that transformed my life. He held my hand and he sent his servants to watch over me and my children. I had people sleeping on the floor of the waiting room those first few nights. I was in a spiritual battle and I needed all the help I could get. The presence of God was so powerful in my life during the year of Tom's accident. Someone once told me we have to practice our faith muscles at calm times so we will be prepared for the storms of life. My faith saved me during my storm and I praise God for his presence in my life.

Late one evening Tom was visited by a councilwoman from Fontana, Aquanetta Warren, who also worked for the city of Upland. She was so kind and let me know that they prayed for Tom at her council meeting.

She said, "I don't care if someone is offended; this man needs some prayer and we are going to pray." It makes you think what would happen if we prayed more in public forums. Another angel that day.

The first day that Tom was able to talk, one of his good friends came into the hospital room and he smiled and said hello. The day before Tom's accident, Scott Griffin had had his own life-threatening scare with a ruptured appendix while vacationing in Mammoth. He had been hospitalized in Mammoth during Tom's accident and had finally made it back home. He had only heard about Tom's condition second-hand and this was the first time he saw Tom in person. As he walked into the room, Tom was sitting up and instantly recognized Scott. Scott broke down and cried, relieved that he knew him and that Tom was going to be okay. Scott said, "Buddy, when you get out of this place, we are going to have a beer." Tom commented that he had turned in his beer for a Bible and would rather spend his time thanking God. Scott was overjoyed. Within days, Scott's wife, Lisa, made sure Tom would hold true to that statement and offered to buy him a Bible. I assured her that Tom had one by his bed.

When I realized Tom was going to be hospitalized for a while, I began to strategize how I was going to raise my children, pay the bills, take care of Tom, and still manage to work. Obviously, I needed to step out on faith with my finances and my time. I knew that I needed to take care of Tom. He was my priority. I have always tithed and given to others in need and never expected anyone to give me anything in return. I never had an expectation that I was entitled to anything. Therefore I figured that I needed to strategize ways to find the financial means to take care of my family. If I wasn't working and with Tom on disability, we would be losing about 60 percent of our income. In addition, I would have increased expenses with a gardener, pool maintenance, and additional childcare expenses as Tom and I would not be available. The scenario didn't look good. It wasn't in my nature to ask for help, but I was scared and concerned. I also began to think of the long-term expenses and became overwhelmed. During that time period, my children were absent a father and only had a mother part time. A traumatic injury disrupts a family in ways that you cannot comprehend until you have experienced it for yourself.

I never really had the opportunity to trust God with my finances. Tom and I had always worked hard, saved our money, and lived a life not only within our means but probably below them. Money had never been a worry for me in our marriage, until now. I was very scared. I am a little embarrassed now that I didn't think I could ask for help and even more so that I wasn't trusting God with this area of my life. As a result of the fundraisers, the support from family, and fellow firefighters taking over Tom's jobs around the house, we not only had enough to pay our bills, but had more in our savings than before the accident by the time Tom and I both returned to work. God fulfilled His promise that He would take care of us. God promises that if we tithe, He will protect our finances. This experience truly changed my perspective of giving. I don't hold onto my money as tight as I did before the accident. I still try to be a good steward, but I am far more giving than I was before. I am also happier with my finances than I have ever been before in my life.

The day before the litigation was over I decided to start giving God praise for the victory. I know we hadn't received it yet, but I knew it was coming. Just like the night I starting praising God for healing Tom when he was still in a coma, I began praising God for the victory in our court case. Rebecca, Catie, and I all held hands in the living room and thanked God for the victory. We chose to thank Him in advance. What a powerful testimony for my children when I called them the next day and let them know that, in fact, it was over, and that we were victorious.

When I see people struggling in their daily lives, I tell them about how God has taught me to be content in all things. Not to be tossed around by the circumstances of my life, but to base my peace on my relationship with the Lord. That is freedom, the freedom that I believe Martin Luther King was talking about in his, "I Have a Dream Speech," the freedom that comes from reconciliation with God. When you are in total submission to God's will, you truly are free. No one can take that from you. It does put life's daily challenges into perspective.

Tom Barilla

When I was at Casa Colina and realized I was badly injured, I remember asking God for strength and for God to protect my wife and children. As time went on and my condition began to get worse, I used to ask why this happened to me. I tried to humanize it and wonder what purpose this was serving. Knowing the power of God, you can't really understand it. When people starting telling me that I wasn't able to go back to work, I began to wonder how I was going to provide for my family. I asked God for guidance, understanding, and protection. I repeated the Lord's Prayer constantly, when I was receiving painful procedures, lying in bed, and during my rehabilitation. One day my pastor came to see me at the hospital and he kept telling me I was a miracle. I remember rubbing what was left of my head and telling him it didn't feel so good to be a miracle.

When I started getting better, I tried to show people the power of God. It was now a testimony and I had to figure out what was going on. I think differently now; I put more thought into all of my decisions. My faith got me through my accident and the lawsuit. It was where I could openly ask for help. You don't need a bus accident to have faith. I have been given a gift, my life. I am not going to take this gift for granted. I didn't earn this gift; it was given to me. I can and never will do anything worthy enough for this gift. I can't answer why I was saved and not someone else. That is why I am building my relationship with God and enjoying every breath I have been given.

Chapter 9: *Rehabilitation*

Yea, though I walk through the valley of death,
I will fear no evil; for You are with me.
Your rod and Your staff, they comfort me.
PSALMS 23:4

WANTED TOM OUT OF THE HOSPITAL AS QUICKLY AS POSSIBLE. HE hated being at Casa Colina. Although it was a wonderful hospital and the people working there were great, there is nothing like being at home. The case manager from the workman's compensation insurance company and I worked as a team to get Tom well since the day Tom was injured. Once I realized her job was to minimize costs while ensuring Tom was well-cared for, we worked together beautifully to make sure Tom recovered optimally. Hers was one of the thirty cards I was given that first day in the hospital. Little did I know how instrumental she would be in Tom's long-term care.

Most people rehabilitating from a traumatic injury experience the opposite of my situation. Their insurance runs out before they are ready to leave the hospital. My problem was that I wanted Tom to leave the hospital but the insurance would continue to pay for him to stay. But that didn't matter to me; once Tom became medically stable, I wanted him to come home. I could take care of him better at home and I could also be with my daughters. My girls had been through such trauma and I wanted to be there for them, and I also knew people were becoming weary staying with Tom at the hospital.

JOHN RUPPERT:
For the next few weeks, I spent a lot of time alone. I had just moved into my house a week before the accident, so I spent most of my time at my house, keeping my mind busy, finding things to do. I went back and forth to the doctor and to my physical therapist and was

released back to work. Joel was still out on injury and Tom was being moved to Casa Colina. Every shift was different; I had an overtime captain and an overtime engineer. I did not like going to visit with Tom on my off days, but I went anyways. He looked like Tom, his voice sounded like Tom . . . but it was not Tom. He spoke softly, slowly, had to think before he said anything, and he moved slowly. Tom is loud, strong spoken, talkative, opinionated, assertive, high energy, never sitting still. It was very hard for me to see him, hard to be in the room with him, knowing he might never get back to his "normal" self.

We explored a Transitional Living Unit at the rehabilitation hospital, but I did not see that as an acceptable alternative. It was a part of rehabilitation where Tom could live and it was more like a home. The problem was that I was not allowed to stay with him. He needed me, not a Transitional Living Unit. Tom and I toured the unit to see if it was an alternative along with my fourteen-year-old niece, Kristyn, who was visiting that day. After the tour and explanation of the services, even in his impaired condition, Tom took the brochure and threw it in the trash and said, "No way in hell am I going there; it is a step above prison." My niece pleaded with me not to put her Uncle Tom in that unit. I didn't know what to do. I finally had to agree, this unit was not an option. I am sure it served a purpose for some patients, but it was not the right place for Tom and we all knew it. I went home that night and cried myself to sleep.

I spent the next day making phone calls to every contact I had in my phone book. A professor at Loma Linda University had given me her card and mentioned that if I needed any help in choosing facilities to call her. I left her a message and she immediately called me back with multiple recommendations. She told me about a facility in Encino that specialized in rehabilitating high level professionals after a traumatic brain injury. I diligently researched every recommendation and went back to Casa Colina with alternative plans of care.

I was very happy with the services that Casa Colina had provided, but I wanted Tom home with me. They were afraid that I wouldn't be able to care for him. After all, brain injury patients can become violent and I might not be able to handle him. We worked together with our physician and came up with a care plan for a trial home visit. If that went well, he could be released and I could bring him back to Casa Colina during the day for rehabilitation. The home visit did go well and Tom was released from the hospital the next week on the condition I would bring him back for daily therapy Monday through Friday.

Those five months of rehabilitation were challenging. I often wonder how I survived, but I did. I put one foot in front of the other, even when I felt like crying on the bathroom floor all day. I did find moments, and hung onto the good things that happened during tragedies. I use to talk to some of the patients while Tom was in therapy and became inspired by their courage. Most people in rehabilitation hospitals have suffered from tragedies worse than most of us can imagine. I worked in the rehabilitation department at Children's Hospital Los Angeles for two years in the 1980s and witnessed multiple tragedies to children, yet now I was looking through a different set of glasses. I couldn't clock out at five o'clock and lead my normal life. None of us could. We were all trapped in what seemed like a time continuum waiting.

The faith that so many patients exhibited was inspiring. So many people couldn't walk, talk, eat, think, or complete daily activities, but they didn't feel sorry for themselves. They had their moments of self-pity, but they couldn't stay there for very long in rehabilitation. Regardless of where they were in their journey of healing, they were moving forward in rehabilitation. The mind is a powerful thing. I used to tell Tom, "you can't do that today, but tomorrow you will." I never let anyone tell Tom he couldn't do something. One case manager was very negative and we ended up getting rid of him. I wasn't about to tolerate anyone telling us we couldn't do something. I have always hated limiting beliefs and it came in handy for this part of the journey. They wanted Tom to take a class titled, "Adjustments to Your Disabilities." I told them that wasn't appropriate and took him out. No one was going to have Tom settle at this point. We didn't even know what his disabilities were; how could we adjust to them?

I watched other patients with brain injuries who didn't have an advocate for them and I wondered what limits were being placed on them. It is not that anyone was intentionally limiting these patients, but there is something to be said for having an advocate who won't accept anything but the best for the patient.

We were also offered a neuropsychologist to help us adjust to the accident, but in all honesty, I think it was too soon. We were focused on getting Tom's physical health back in place and the emotional healing wouldn't begin for at least a year. On a follow-up visit a few months after Tom finished therapy, our physician asked if we needed any counseling. We told him that we didn't think we needed it, but we thanked him. Our doctor commented that our faith would probably heal us just as much as therapy, but to let him know if we needed any further help.

When Tom and I began having challenges adjusting back to our relationship, we opted to see a Christian marriage counselor from our church. We visited him a few times several years after the accident, but I wish we would have spent more time dealing with the emotional aspect of Tom's brain injury. As much as everyone tried to prepare us for what was to come, we really could have used a support system for the weird challenges that came with the injury. We were probably a little too quick to be released from care. I think we were so glad Tom was healed physically that we didn't want to think about it anymore than we had to. Believe me, it is not a weakness to seek help for the emotional aspect of an injury; it is wise.

After five months in daily therapy, Tom and I wanted to be finished so badly. It was a long tedious process and we experienced many emotions. We were so grateful to all of the therapists, especially those who really cared and gave that extra. They do God's work here on earth. I know it isn't always easy, but what a service they provide to so many people who would have been written off in the years past. I often wonder what would have happened to Tom had he not had the aggressive therapy with their dedication to get him back to work. Even if they didn't believe he would ever go back to work, we appreciated them playing along with us. For those who were negative and didn't believe in us, I would ask that they spend some time in reflection, wondering why they were in rehabilitation; perhaps another career might be suitable.

JOHN RUPPERT:
One day after work, Big Ed Weaver and I went together to visit Tom at Casa Colina. He was in the middle of his physical therapy, sitting in his wheelchair, working out his legs. We stood there with Dora and watched him from a distance for a while. When he looked up

and saw us, he smiled, missing teeth and deformed skull in a doo-rag. Ed and I chatted with Tom for a while when he made some comment, another one of his one liners, and it made us all laugh. It was the first time that I had truly smiled at Tom since the accident. I don't remember what he said, but it was funny, it was perfectly timed . . . Tom was back.

When people are at their lowest in life, they need to be lifted up and encouraged that they can accomplish anything. Without that belief, they will never move forward. It is just too easy to remain victims and never move beyond their injuries.

Chapter 10: *Humor — Laughter Really is Good Medicine*

A cheerful heart is good medicine,
but a crushed spirit dries up the bones.
PROVERBS 17:22

TOM USED TO ALWAYS TEASE ME AND SAY THAT WHEN WE GOT TO heaven, God was going to tell us that we took it all way too seriously and that we should have just laughed more and enjoyed life. Humor is a coping mechanism that Tom mastered a long time ago. He often reminded me of Hawkeye in *Mash* who joked about the most horrific situations as a way of coping.

Although Tom was in a coma for the first twelve days following the accident, his humorous remarks filled the waiting room of the hospital, as his co-workers would mimic his humorous lines. We all found a compassionate laughter that emerged as we shared this horrible tragedy. It was a common place for all of us, where humor was interwoven with tragedy. I felt so grateful for those moments. It was as if pressure were being released from my soul and it allowed me to breathe.

There was a book in the hospital waiting room for visitors to write their thoughts to Tom. A few of the journal entries read:

"Get well . . . soon! I want to hear more of your jokes really soon."

"I believe in God and the Lord Jesus Christ, and I believe that God has a plan. I pray and hope for you, Tom, and your family that his plan will be revealed to you. That Tom will be Tom, 'The King of the one-liners,' again. That this will be a story of amazing strength, courage, and hope . . . Tick tock, Tom, Tic Tock."

Tom was known as the king of one-liners and those one-liners made us laugh even when he was unconscious. I hated some of those one-liners. Tom used to use a phrase "Wud-up" in an annoying voice — translated as "what is up." I used to tell Tom not to use that line on me because it was repulsive. As I sat there watching him, all I could think of was how grateful I would be when he could look at me and say "Wud-up" with that sarcastic smirk.

Additional journal entries went on to say . . .

> *"I have to say you are the only member of our department that has had a smile on his face every time I see you come to work. You may not realize how your smile helps make the rest of us having a bad day, have a much better one simply from your smile."*

> *"I think it is the carburetor." (Apparently this was an inside joke)*

Often times in the waiting room people would project what Tom was thinking as a way to break the tension. In the midst of a tremendous crisis, Tom was making us laugh. It felt good to laugh while waiting for his numerous surgeries or sitting by his unconscious bedside for countless hours. It was a healthy break from the endless tears I seemed to shed.

Several weeks after the accident I was attempting to get the girls off to school and became overwhelmed with the tasks in front of me for the day. I thought about one of Tom's one-liners: "Dora, if you're not laughing, you're crying." I had cried enough, thank God for laughter.

JOHN RUPPERT, RECALLING THE FIRST TIME HE MET TOM:
"Hi John, I'm Tom Barilla; nice to meet you," Tom said as he stretched out his hand to mine. On the other side of the desk sat Captain Cascadden, who introduced himself, with a firm handshake as, "Joel Cascadden." He did not say he was a captain, but he did not have to. He had that presence about him that most men in leadership positions have. He sat back quietly, observing, dissecting, with a serious look on his face. Tom, on the other hand, was a fireman. He was loud, talkative, and energetic, keeping the atmosphere light. I remember thinking that if he had an east coast accent, he could have been a perfect fit with FDNY. I was nervous and intimidated,

but thankful to be there. This was only my second interview with a fire department. I was a year out of the fire academy, applying for the position of reserve firefighter. I had very little experience in the emergency medical field, six months as an EMT, and I had no fire experience to speak of. I can't remember what I was asked, or how well I did during the interview; I only remember the question that I could not answer. But I knew the answer; I was an EMT, working on an ambulance for the last six months. I knew the answer . . . just not on that day. The question that Tom had asked was, "What does S.T.A.R.T. stand for?" I felt like an idiot. I could not answer that question; I had completely blanked out. I gave the standard reply people give when they do not know, "I cannot think of it right now, but I will find out and be able to answer it next time, sir." "Next time," I thought, "ha!" There wouldn't be a next time, I was ruined. START. Simple Triage and Rapid Transport. Rapid Transport is so important in trauma patients. The chances of survivability seem to be directly related to how fast the patient receives treatment at a trauma hospital.

When Tom started coming out of his coma on day ten, he had that smile on his face. At one point he farted and although he couldn't talk, he looked at me smiled and shook his head and I could hear him saying, "Umm-hmm." I laughed so hard.

When Tom started to speak, although his mind was not yet cognizant, he was still telling relevant jokes. I had read in the literature that traumatic brain injury patients became violent and were verbally abusive. Not Tom; he continued joking with his nurses, his visitors, and his family with that big smile on his face. Tom may not have been able to articulate an intelligent question, but his humor was still intact.

When he was transferred to the rehabilitation hospital, Tom went through extensive neurological testing. I found it ironic that the part of the brain that he injured was related to his ability to interpret humor. When I was asked if his humor function appeared to be affected, I just laughed and told the psychologist that not even a bus could kill that in Tom.

During Tom's rehabilitation at Casa Colina, I would go home at night to be with the girls and get them off to school every day. We had a group of about six people who would stay with Tom during the night. One morning I received a call from his brother Paul who had spent the previous night with him and said that Tom wanted to talk to me. As he handed the phone to Tom, I heard heavy breathing on the other end of the phone. I wondered if Tom was having difficulty breathing and began to be concerned. Within a few seconds Paul was back on the line. When I questioned him about the strange noises I heard on the other line, he replied that Tom missed me and he was breathing sexy through the tracheotomy hole in his neck that had not yet healed. Only Tom would think to do something that outrageous. Paul and I laughed hysterically. Where did he get his material?

When Tom was in Casa Colina his humor began to return in full force. When patients needed a nurse, they would use a call button that made this annoying buzzing sound, and Tom would continually remark, "the cookies are done." This became an ongoing joke for anyone visiting and even for some of the nursing staff.

Speech therapy at Casa Colina entailed questions that would make Tom work his brain, which got him so confused and frustrated. He had the same therapist every day and when we saw her in the hallways, Tom would say, "Kelly, I can't wait till our mind games at eleven o'clock; see you there."

One morning Joel called and said that the department was having a ceremony for John Ruppert, the fireman in the accident with Tom, who was getting off his one-year probation. This was just a formality; we all knew John had passed his test the morning of the accident — he went from being a boy to a man on March 15, 2005. Joel wondered if we could drop by to say hello and needless to say, I was motivated to show my gratitude to someone who helped save my husband's life that day.

I knew Tom couldn't handle a lot of stimulus, so we agreed to stop by after the ceremony, but would only stay for a few minutes. Tom refused to wear his helmet inside the station and put on a doo-rag. He still looked pretty bad but he was able to walk in. Before they put Tom's skull back together, he had to wear a helmet to protect his brain. After all, without the bone, there was nothing to protect his brain from further damage. I was a nervous wreck when he wasn't wearing his helmet. He was toothless with a dented head, stitches, and still skin and bones, but it didn't matter. When he walked in the room people were overjoyed to see him. Everyone wanted to talk to him and take their pictures with Tom. Tom began making jokes because he knew he looked pathetic. He started holding a cup and asking for "money for the cripple," and "extra for pictures in front of the fire engine." Even with his brain impaired, he knew he looked awful and made light of the situation so people wouldn't feel sorry for him. He didn't want their pity, he wanted to pay his gratitude to John. That was a painful morning for me and I was so thankful for the humor.

Chapter 11: *Going Home*

From everyone who has been given much, much
will be demanded; and from the one who has been
entrusted with much, much more will be asked.
LUKE 12:48

REBECCA BARILLA:

We had to move my sister Catie's room before my dad came home.
We also had to change things so Dad could come home. We put bars
in the bathroom and stuff on the floor so he wouldn't slip. I was so
glad he was coming home and I wanted to do anything.

THE MORNING I BROUGHT TOM HOME FROM BEING AN INPATIENT at the hospital, about four fire engines and three police cars were waiting at our home to give Tom a big welcome. I was so touched by their continued thoughtfulness and Tom was completely overwhelmed. Tom had been given explicit instructions to wear his helmet in the car, as he still did not have his skull covering his head and the slightest bump could cause significant brain damage. As we drove up to the driveway and Tom saw his fellow firefighters, he began to take off his helmet. Knowing we still had to walk into the house, I was horrified of him falling. I had nightmares about Tom hitting his head on everyday objects and tended to be a little overprotective. Getting Tom to see the danger of not wearing the helmet wasn't as easy.

Tom was allowed to come home from Casa Colina with the agreement that I would take him back for outpatient therapy everyday, but he was home now and had no intention of going back. Unfortunately, he was far from ready to stop his rehabilitation. The next morning I woke up my two daughters, got them ready for school and then tried to wake up Tom to get him ready for his full day of rehabilitation. Tom had other plans and wasn't about to get out of bed and began to yell at me for being so cruel. Joel called me that morning to see how things were going. I began to cry and tell him I couldn't do this. I shouldn't have taken Tom home so soon. I was crying, Tom was yelling, and my children were horrified. I wondered if this was my new life.

Coming home was another challenge in our journey. Tom wanted me to be by his side every moment. I can only imagine how alone, afraid, and vulnerable Tom must have felt. I know if I had been in his shoes I would not want Tom to leave me alone for a second, but I felt like I was being smothered. I needed a break. At times the walls felt like they were closing in on me. I would leave the house and if I was gone longer than an hour, Tom would be calling me asking when I would be home. I was so torn. I loved knowing he was home, but I needed a break every once in a while. My life was spinning out of control and the four walls only made me dizzy. I had so many questions that no one could answer.

I still had support from close friends but after a while people had to return to their lives and I was soon all alone. I felt as though I had the whole world on my shoulders. I contemplated taking some of Tom's pain medication the first week he was home because my emotional pain was more than I could bear. I thank God I opted against that choice and prayed to God instead.

I managed to find some routine and normalcy to my new chaotic life. Each day I took my girls to school and came back to get Tom out of bed and take him to Casa Colina. Each day I parked in a handicap space and pulled out Tom's wheelchair to push him into his therapy. I hated the wheelchair and felt sorry for myself often. Wasn't Tom supposed to take care of me? Shouldn't he be opening the door for me? Instead I was lugging his wheelchair out of my car every day and pushing him around. It was exhausting and made the simplest trip a long journey. I used to watch an older woman do the same thing for her husband who had had a stroke fifteen years prior. How had she done this for fifteen years? She must have been a saint. It reminded me that no matter how bad my situation appeared, there was always someone in a worse situation. It did seem to put things in perspective. As time went on, I stopped feeling sorry for myself and eventually grabbing the wheelchair became second nature.

Tom Barilla:

When Dora would put me in the car, I knew I was physically unable to help her with the wheelchair. As I sat in the car, I would adjust the rearview mirror and watch her struggle to put the wheelchair away. I felt helpless and I used it as a motivation to get better. It was a constant reminder of what a burden I was to my wife. It made me so angry. I vowed I would get better.

When Tom returned home I wondered if our relationship would ever be the same. Would we ever be able to be intimate again? Could he? We were told that the brain injury might affect our intimacy. It seemed pretty irrelevant at the time, but my mind did wander. Tom must have wondered himself; he wanted to make sure everything worked a few weeks after he came home. It did, but our sex life was different. The stress of the injury and lawsuit along with my recent weight gain created a lot of mental barriers. It took years before our sex life returned to a sense of normalcy, but once it did it was better than before.

Chapter 12:
Healing is Not a Linear Process

He asked this only to test him, for he already
had in mind what he was going to do.
JOHN 6:6

OM'S MONTHS OF REHABILITATION AFTER THE ACCIDENT INCLUD-
ED DAILY sessions of physical, speech, and occupational therapy. We
had multiple therapists, physicians, specialists, and prosthodontists
literally putting Tom back together again. Healing from a brain injury
is similar to taking care of a child. Tom had to relearn everything. For
weeks we changed his diaper, fed him, taught him to sit up, walk, and
eventually talk and think critically.

Our physiatrist at Casa Colina told us that healing from a brain injury was not a linear process. That was one of the best pieces of advice I
received. Although it generally was forward moving, we had some real
setbacks that were very discouraging and felt like progress was at a stand-
still. When I look back and think about it, the lulls weren't that long, but
at the time they seemed like an eternity. While everyone else was moving
on with their lives, I was stuck in my bubble. I felt like a hamster in one
of those wheels, feverishly running to get somewhere but never getting
anywhere.

At this point Tom still didn't have the top of his skull back in place,
so I continued to treat him like a china doll. He hated wearing the helmet because it made his head sweat and it was terribly uncomfortable.
He took it off every chance he had, which made me a nervous wreck. He
asked me to get him a doo-rag to protect his head and help prevent the
sweat. I didn't even know what a doo-rag was. After a little research I
realized it was the head covering used by motorcyclists to protect their
heads. My search for doo-rags became a little comical in our family and

everyone began looking for them as well. I eventually had more doo-rags than I needed. My daughter Catie and my nephew Tyler thought they were pretty cool and asked for one. Doo-rags became a fashion around our neighborhood that year.

While Tom was still an inpatient at Casa Colina, he needed to have the wiring removed from his mouth. Tom was so happy, as the wiring tore holes on the inside of his mouth and made it very difficult to eat anything. Tom was thin even before the accident and had lost over thirty pounds since. He was so skinny it was frightening. Arrowhead Regional Medical Center made an appointment to remove the wires at their dental clinic. I opted to drive Tom myself as the other alternative was to have an ambulance transport him back to the hospital. He wore his helmet, but I still drove like an old lady.

I brought Tom up to the dental clinic at the county facility in his wheelchair and began to feel nauseous in the waiting room. We waited for a long time and finally we were brought back to the exam rooms. I stood outside the exam room because it was too crowded. While they worked on Tom a few prisoners in handcuffs and chains walked past me in the hallway. This couldn't be happening. My husband was receiving dental care right next to prisoners. It never occurred to me that the county facility would be the place where prisoners received their care. It was a very unsettling experience. I went home that evening and vomited all night. I don't know if I was physically ill or if it was my body's way of purging the stress I had experienced over the past several weeks.

After my experience at Arrowhead Regional Medical Center, I made it my top priority to identify a private prosthodontist, the specialist pertaining to the diagnosis, treatment planning, rehabilitation and maintenance of the oral function, comfort, appearance and health of patients with clinical conditions associated with missing or deficient teeth and/or oral and maxillofacial tissues using biocompatible substitute; in other words, a dentist who could put Tom's teeth and mouth back together. Before Tom's surgery I didn't even know that a prosthodontist existed.

Luckily I found a prosthodontist in LaVerne, Tony Daher, who was also on faculty in the school of dentistry at Loma Linda University School of Dentistry. This had to be a better option; I couldn't bear to return to the dental clinic at the county facility. LaVerne was only five minutes from the rehabilitation hospital, so we wouldn't have to miss our daily therapy. I was so glad that we chose someone close because it took months rebuilding his mouth. It was a very long and arduous process.

With all of the other surgeries he was asleep, but with all of his dental work, Tom was wide awake. Tom will tell you that his dental work was the most painful. Basically, his mouth was reconstructed; his entire face had practically been rebuilt. There is so much titanium in place, his X-ray looks like he is a robot. Tom's upper mouth did not have the bone structure to support implants so he opted to have bridges to replace his teeth. I think Tom would have chosen this option anyways as he has declared he would never have another surgery in his life. Tom continues to have more problems with his teeth than anything else besides the headaches. The upkeep is constant and a daily reminder of the accident. He is unable to determine if something is hot and does not have any sensation, making many daily functions an ongoing challenge.

After weeks of rehabilitation Tom began to have a decline in the movement on his left side. Tom is left-handed and began to struggle to sign in for therapy everyday. Fortunately his occupational therapist was very responsive to our concern in his paralysis and began aggressive treatment immediately. She was one of my favorite people and we had a great relationship. In spite of the therapy the paralysis began to worsen every day. Tom could no longer hold a fork, shave, or open a door with his left hand. He was tested for just about everything; even carpal tunnel was considered. He wore a wrist band for months, but nothing seemed to help. The paralysis only worsened each day. He was referred to a hand specialist, but we were unable to get appointments in the morning and began to see the therapist in the evening. One night when taking Tom to his appointment, I began to notice that he was limping on the left side. His leg was beginning to drag. Tom was in denial that anything was wrong. He just said he was tired and I was just looking for things to be wrong with him.

REBECCA BARILLA:
When Dad couldn't use his left hand at dinner, we all used our other hands to eat so he wouldn't feel so bad.

I remember informing the hand therapist of the progressive paralysis on the left side and she was the first to acknowledge that it might be due to the brain injury. I remember looking in her eyes and knowing that she was right. I couldn't stop the tears and it was as though a floodgate was opened. I wasn't crying out loud, but the tears were flowing uncontrollably. I felt bad for the therapist. I am sure that she thought she made me cry, but it was just the realization that what she was saying was true. Tom wasn't getting better; he was getting worse. Now we needed to be realistic. He was paralyzed on his left side and the paralysis began to progress with each day.

I called his brother Mike and Joel, his captain, over the next day to look at Tom and confirm what I had suspected. Both of them denied my suspicion. I often wonder if they were both in denial or if they didn't notice the subtle changes because they weren't with him every minute of the day. They both just said he was probably tired and he needed sleep and it would go away. Now I felt like I was going crazy. Was it just me? Was I looking for things to be wrong with Tom? For the next couple of weeks I continued to watch Tom's paralysis progress and felt completely helpless; neither of us talked about it because it was just too painful. His healing was now regressing and I was becoming very discouraged. This was the loneliest and most frustrating part of his recovery. Everyone was helping Tom to adjust to his disability and I was refusing to accept the reality.

I searched long and hard for someone to help me. I was given a referral for a neurologist while Tom was still in a coma at Arrowhead Regional Medical Center, but the doctor was not in the country at the time, so I had forgotten about him. I decided I was going to need a neurologist to oversee Tom's care and probably needed to find someone we both liked. Tom and I now refer to Dr. Kenneth Jordan as our saving grace. He had the bedside manner of a saint. He was so kind, professional, and knowledgeable. He ordered a follow-up MRI for Tom and instantly identified the source of Tom's paralysis. He didn't even hesitate; he showed us the MRI and said that the skin from his head had grown to the Dura of the brain, putting pressure on the right side of the brain, causing paralysis to the left side. They had left the skull unattached for too long. Dr. Jordan said that once the bone was put back in place, it would relieve the pressure on the brain and he should regain mobility. Finally an answer that made sense. We had hope again. I aggressively pursued scheduling the surgery for Tom's skull to be replaced.

It turned out I wasn't crazy. The hand therapist was right. The paralysis was due to his brain injury. We finally had an answer. Having the correct diagnosis brought relief to Tom and me that was equivalent to a lifetime of stressors. We both knew we still had many hills to climb, but paralysis on the left side of his body wasn't one of them. The healing process could now move forward with optimism.

Chapter 13: *The Miracle and Support After Surgery*

He is your God, the one who is worthy of your praise, the one who has done mighty miracles that you yourselves have seen.
DEUTERONOMY 10:21

DAILY BULLETIN
RECOVERING FIREFIGHTER ON HIS FEET
(Original pub. date: 6/24/2005)
Sara A. Carter, Staff Writer

RANCHO CUCAMONGA — *The Epicenter was truly a field of dreams Thursday night.*

Upland fire engineer Tom Barilla stood proudly with his two daughters and wife on the mound preparing to do something miraculous — pitch a ball. And to the cheers of fans in the stadium, the recovering firefighter threw a strike for the ceremonial pitch.

The 40-year-old 2004 Upland Firefighter of the Year was near death March 15 after a bus plowed into his fire engine in the carpool lane of the 10 Freeway while the engine was responding to a traffic accident.

Barilla suffered major head and chest injuries when he was ejected from the vehicle and was not expected to survive.

"They told me I should have been in a coma or dead," said Tom Barilla from the dugout before the pitch. "But when I woke up and saw (my daughters) by my bedside, that was it. I knew I had to go on. It's just a miracle."

Barilla's wife, Dora Barilla, never gave up hope on her husband. She took a leave of absence from her job as a health consultant and has stayed by his side through his ongoing recovery, which has included several surgeries and weeks of rehabilitation.

"The power of prayer is what really saved him," Dora Barilla said. "I think tragedies like this bring out the best in humanity. Sometimes we forget how to give, how to love, until something like this happens and then we remember the power of community."

For the past three months, the Barilla family has been showered by the kindness of strangers, including some whom Barilla himself aided over his 14 years on the job.

Assemblyman Bill Emmerson, R-Redlands and San Bernardino County Supervisor Paul Biane, who hosted the Firefighter and Law Enforcement Tribute Night, said the event was the community's way of saying "thank you" to the men and women who put their lives on the line daily to protect the public.

"We're really happy to hear about the progress he's making," Biane said. "Our firefighters are always doing such a great job and miracles like this don't happen often enough."

Law enforcement and fire personnel from Fontana, Rancho Cucamonga, Upland, and Ontario attended the game free of charge and a percentage of ticket sales was donated to Barilla's family. A silent auction of sports memorabilia was also held in the concourse to raise money for the family.

But for Rebecca, 10, and Catie, 7, their father's life was the greatest treasure of all.

"It felt so good," Rebecca said with a smile. "I liked being out on the field because I was out there with my daddy."

The day of the accident, a casino tour bus, traveling eastbound in the carpool lane of the 10, collided with the left rear of the fire engine, causing it to rotate counterclockwise, according to officials from the California Highway Patrol.

One bus passenger, Kau Leung, 75, was killed and dozens, including two other firefighters, were hurt. All the injured, except for Barilla, were later released from local hospitals.

Barilla is still recovering from his injuries and underwent cranial surgery last Friday. His ability to bounce back is amazing, his wife said.

And his strength gives others hope, said Rancho Cucamonga Fire Chief Peter Bryan.

"In my 30-year career, I have never seen such a miracle," Bryan said. "He's an inspiration to everyone."

DORA'S JOURNAL ENTRY MARCH 20, 2005

Thank you, Lord, for Tom's miracle. Today Tom is in critical condition. It is six days from the accident. I am praising God he is alive. He is still not responsive. He has a trach, two tubes in one lung and that horrible bolt in his head. It is now a waiting game. My heart is aching, but I am holding on to the miracle. We are praying against infection and for the bolt, tubes, and assistance ventilation to be removed. The miracle will be complete when we know his brain is intact. My other prayer is to comfort and guide Rebecca and Catie.

ISN'T IT AMAZING THAT GOD WILL BE SO FAITHFUL IN SO MANY WAYS, yet we forget all that when one thing goes wrong. I was given a journal while Tom was in a coma and told to journal his progress and remember the healing each day. I enjoy reading that journal entry because it reminds me of what I have been given.

When our third round of surgeries were about to begin, I needed to remember the miracles I had been given in the past. Tom's surgery was scheduled for June 17, 2005, approximately three months after his skull had been removed and the swelling in his brain had subsided. We returned to Arrowhead Regional Medical Center where his skull was still in their freezer. We went in early that morning with our Pastor, Steve DeYoung, and we prayed in the waiting area for Tom's complete recovery. I remember the peace I had that morning. Although there were only a few people waiting with me, I knew that Tom was covered in prayer.

The firefighters with their heads shaved.

The night before Tom's surgery about ten firemen shaved their heads to show their love and support for Tom. What a great gesture. If nothing else, the picture made me laugh. It was spearheaded by the firefighter who was in the accident with Tom. I always wondered why people shaved their heads when their loved ones had cancer; now I knew. People needed to do something when there was nothing they could do. It was a reminder to let people do things for me and not pretend like I didn't need help. Helping was as much about their healing as it was about ours. When Tom went into surgery to have his skull replaced it was very different. My angels stayed with me all the way until the end. I still look at the picture of the bald fireman and smile.

The surgery lasted a few hours and I was allowed to go back into recovery to see Tom. It was a little painful to see him with his head shaved and bandaged again. Although he was recognizable, it was still challenging to experience this all over again. I hated seeing him unconscious. It brought back so much pain. I didn't leave his side. We were moved into a private room on the floor. My grandfather had gone in for surgery that same day and my mom was in northern California, so my sister was with our girls. At Tom's request, no one came to visit that evening. I sat in the chair next to Tom all night. It was absolutely freezing and Tom got up all night to try to go to the bathroom. He had a catheter during surgery and he had the sensation to urinate all night and I was so afraid he was going to fall and hurt his head. Another long, lonely, and cold night.

In the morning, my least favorite neurosurgeon resident came to remove the tube in Tom's head. I must have been tired because he asked me to leave the room and I did. I am glad I did, because Tom said he pulled a two-foot tube out of his head and he didn't use much grace in doing it, and then just stapled the opening without any anesthesia. I probably would have decked him had I watched, so it was best I wasn't there. When I returned to the room the doctor gave me instructions on caring for his wound. Tom had over fifty staples in his head and the doctor was concerned about infection. He said Tom would be in terrible shape if it got infected, so I had to be sure to clean it and put the ointment on it often.

Once we recovered from the trauma of the neurosurgeon resident's visit, Tom realized that his paralysis was beginning to subside. We went home that day and the healing process was on the upswing once again.

Within a week of his surgery, we were invited to a baseball game at our local triple A baseball stadium. The community was having another fundraiser for Tom and honoring local firefighters. They asked if Tom would consider throwing out the first pitch of the game. Tom was determined and practiced all week throwing a baseball with the hand that was paralyzed just two weeks prior.

Our entire family went to the baseball game that night. Most of them weren't able to come for Tom's surgery and they were anxious to see how

Tom throwing out the first pitch at Quakes stadium.

Tom was recovering. We went down to the field and were welcomed by local politicians and the press. It was the first time the press had a chance to talk to us since his surgery. The girls and I walked out to the pitcher's mound with Tom. We were joined by our local board of supervisors, Paul Biane, and our local assemblyman, Bill Emmerson. All three men had been asked to throw out a pitch before the game. The two politicians threw out the first two pitches. Then it was finally Tom's turn. He got up to the plate and the crowd cheered as though they had just watched Babe Ruth hit a home run. When he threw out the pitch, their cheers sent chills down my spine. I thought it sounded like angels cheering in heaven, reminding me that God completed the great works that he began in us. The next day Tom was on the front page of the local paper with his shaved head and fifty stitches throwing out the first pitch with the headline, "Recovering firefighter on his feet: A strike of inspiration."

A week prior Tom was paralyzed and couldn't use his hand at all.

Chapter 14: *Children and Tragedy*

Neither this man nor his parents sinned,
said Jesus, but this happened so that the work
of God might be displayed in his life.
JOHN 9:3

UNFORTUNATELY, I HAD BEEN UNABLE TO PICK UP MY CHILDREN the day of the accident. My friend Jill picked up Catie and Rebecca from elementary school. I asked her not to let them watch TV and let me tell them the details about what had happened.

CATIE BARILLA:

"Why wasn't my mom picking me up?" I felt scared when Jill told me my dad was in an accident. I went in the other room and prayed with my best friend Abby. When my mom came home at 8:00 she asked me if I heard what happened. Then Mom said she was going back to the hospital to take care of dad. We didn't cry because we wanted to be strong for our mom. When she left we cried for an hour with my Aunt Becka. Then we made cards for my dad to hang in his room. The next day the phone kept ringing and my Aunt Becka took us for a walk.

I felt thankful that people helped us. The people in my class brought us food. My teacher brought us chicken. My friend's mom brought us dinner all the time so we could eat at night.

When I saw my dad for the first time in the hospital I was shocked and afraid to touch him. He was all scary. He had a lot of stuff hooked up to him. I think they were tubes. One day in rehabilitation I tried to read him a book and he kept having to go to the bathroom. I just wanted him to come home and be fine. We moved my room when my dad came home. I felt sad because I liked being near my mom and dad. I felt guilty that everyone was moving my stuff. I would tell myself to hang in there and never give up. A lot of people sent flowers. My house smelled great. My mom recorded my voice for my dad.

REBECCA BARILLA:

When Jill first told me my dad was in an accident, I started to cry. Then I went to get my sister and we called my mom on the phone. My mom said Dad has been in an accident and we needed to keep praying for him. I was pretty scared. I remember everyone was staring at me and you could tell they felt sorry for me. Then I walked in the living room and I saw the accident on the TV and it freaked me out because I didn't know how big of an accident it really was and that there was a big chance that my dad might not make it. When my mom came home, we tried not to cry because we wanted to be strong. The second my mom left we just kept crying with my Aunt Becka. We didn't go to school for a while. People started coming to our house and bringing us stuff. Some of the food was really good. We also got a lot of flowers. The flowers made the house smell good and it was nice to know people cared enough about us to send us stuff. I didn't understand why we weren't allowed to go to the hospital for a couple of weeks. I didn't understand what it meant to be in a coma. I was confused. Everyone kept leaving the room when they were talking on the phone. Not knowing was making things worse. Catie and I used to listen at the door so we could know what was going on.

When we first went to the hospital, my Nana took us and I remember wanting to throw up in the car. We went into the hospital and my mom met us in another room to prepare us better for what we were going to see. When we walked in his hospital room, I saw all of the things we made for our dad. Then I saw my dad and I started to cry and I didn't want anyone to see me. My dad couldn't talk yet. My mom talked to him for us because Catie and I were freaked out. We left after that and we came back another day. When my dad could mouth stuff he mouthed I love you and it was kind of sad, but it was also one of those things that made it seem like he was get-

ting better. It also meant that he recognized who we were. My mom warned us that he might not know who we were, but he did. That made me feel better. I remember on Easter all of our family was at the hospital and someone sent us enormous Easter bunnies and we had food with all of our family. My uncle Jim was there and we played cards. I really liked that my family was there in the hospital and that people brought us food.

We made a shirt for my dad from Napoleon Dynamite that said, "It's a sledgehammer," and "You're just jealous, Napoleon, because I have been chatting online with babes all day." Then everyone signed it and we brought it to Dad.

When Dad first went to Casa Colina, my mom kept asking him questions. She asked him what his phone number was and he said 1-800-Crappola. It was funny and it made me laugh. For my mom and dad's anniversary, Lacy and Andrea took us to Build-A-Bear and we made bears that were a bride and a groom and we went to eat at Islands. It was a lot of fun and it was nice to get out of the house and not be at the hospital. That was a good day. Something that I learned during my dad's accident is that pain in inevitable but misery was optional. We overcame his accident as a family, it wasn't easy but we chose to make the best of every situation.

How do you tell your children their father is in critical condition and might not live? I still don't know. I didn't want to lie to them, but I didn't want them be traumatized either. I couldn't be with them to console them. I had to rely on my family to be there for my children. I told both Catie and Rebecca that Daddy had been in an accident and that it was bad and we needed to pray. I did the best I could. I remember that I needed to come home and spend a few minutes with them. I was petrified to leave Tom at the hospital, but my children needed to see me in person to assure them the best I could. The comfort I received holding them in my arms was a breath of fresh air. They gave me the strength I needed to persevere.

I followed the hospital's recommendation not to bring the girls to see their father in that condition, until my ten-year-old daughter told me on the tenth day, "Mommy, you can not keep my daddy from me anymore. I want to see him." That comment was like a brick in my face. I think she was right. I had never been one to question my parenting skills, but this was definitely a scenario I could use some professional help in addressing. I asked Barbie Rice, a lay counselor from my church to come to my home. She was such a blessing. I shared with her my dilemma and what the hospital said. She said that perhaps it was time for the girls to see Tom. She asked me what would happen if God healed Tom? What would that do for my children's faith? They would witness an incredible miracle.

Wow, that was a perspective I hadn't considered. Barbie was right. I made the decision to let the girls see Tom after they removed an ICP tube from Tom's head. It was time to let the girls visit the hospital. It was Good Friday, three days before Easter. My mom picked up the girls from school and she drove them to the hospital. I met them in the waiting room and did my best to prepare them for what they were about to see.

At this point, Tom was slightly conscious and could recognize faces. When the girls entered Tom's room they wouldn't go near his bed. They were afraid. Tom recognized them and you could clearly see a smile when he saw the girls. I never pushed the children to go near Tom and they only stayed in the room for about five minutes. We went back into waiting room and twenty minutes later the girls asked to go back and see their dad. This time they went closer and told Tom they loved him. Rebecca started to cry. Tom made a hand gesture to her that he loved her. We went back to the waiting room. The girls returned the next day and this time they actually touched Tom. We were making progress. The girls posted the get-well cards all over Tom's room and we left.

If the places were reversed for Tom and me, the one thing that would motivate me to live would be to see the faces of my two beautiful children. It was the right decision.

At the time of the accident, my younger sister Becka was living with us. She had made some life decisions that brought her to the lowest point in her life. Up until then, Tom and I had disagreed about the best way to help my sister. I was always trying to protect her and Tom felt she needed to face the consequences of her behavior, but it was hard to see someone I loved so much destroy her life. But in March of 2004, Tom agreed under very certain conditions that it was time to help her. Before she moved in, I yelled at her in frustration to get her life in order and stop being so selfish; I might need her one day and she needed to be healthy. Little did I know how true that statement would be only one year later. My sister spent the year turning her life around while bonding with my children. What a blessing she turned out to be when I needed her the most. Both my sister and my mother stayed with my children around the clock while I was with Tom at the hospital. I wish I could have been there for my children, but I knew they had two people with them who loved them dearly. By the time Tom came home from the hospital, my sister was ready to move out of the house and has since reclaimed her life.

As Catie grew older and we talked about the accident, she often told me that she wished people would have told her more. I thought I was protecting her and I should have talked to her and been more up front. She told me she used to listen at the door to try and figure out what was happening. I learned that if you don't talk to your children, they tend to imagine things are far worse than the truth.

In 2007, I received news that my friend Veronica, who had had battled breast cancer for years, was put in hospice. She had put in a good fight, but at this point the cancer had spread to her brain and treatment was futile. I remember the evening I went to visit Veronica with my two daughters, I prepared them for the reality of Veronica's situation. I explained that hospice meant that Veronica wasn't going to live and the doctors sent her home to die comfortably with her family. My daughter Catie instantly protested my explanation. She told me that everyone thought Dad was going to die, but people prayed and he was healed; I shouldn't be so negative and we should pray for Veronica. My heart sank at her words. I was so grateful for her faith and agreed that I needed to pray for Veronica and that I didn't know how God would work out her illness. Although Veronica went home to be with the Lord later that year, I was amazed at the peace that she had in her death. My children reminded me that we don't know what will happen in all situations, but we needed to pray regardless.

Working through tragedy with your children will model coping skills for them as they experience tragedy in their own lives. Will they have faith and trust God, be open and honest, or will they be closed, afraid, and withdrawn?

Chapter 15:
Preparing to Go Back to Work

For though a righteous man falls seven times, he rises again.
PROVERBS 24:16

DAILY BULLETIN

A REMARKABLE RECOVERY: FIREFIGHTER BADLY INJURED IN CRASH HEADED BACK TO WORK.
8/4/2005

Tom Barilla, an Upland firefighter seriously injured in a traffic accident on the 10 Freeway, is getting his life back to normal after coming out of a coma and undergoing months of physical therapy. In May, firefighter Tom Barilla couldn't write or even hold a pen in his hand. Three months later, the engineer-paramedic is scheduled to begin light duty at the Upland Fire Department, with the eventual goal of going back to firefighting full-time. The August 15 return to work is one more miracle in a parade of miracles since the day of the crash, said Tom and his wife, Dora, who have dubbed their lives as "before the accident" and "after the accident."

So NOW TOM HAD REACHED THE POINT WHERE IT WAS TIME to go back to work. In Tom's mind, that was the ultimate goal. Tom said "I am going to go back to work and give back what so many people have given to me." This was the last step in his journey (so he thought at the time). I was looking for the end of the marathon and this appeared to be the finish line. I had been asking where the finish line was and it was actually here. This entire nightmare could be put to rest and we could move on with our lives.

At the time, Tom did not realize the ambiguity in a brain injury. When you physically injure your body, there are agility tests that can be given to ensure you are capable of performing your physical requirements at your job. When you injure your brain, what are the known and accepted protocols to return to your employment? This part of the journey was one of the most challenging steps in recovery. I wish someone told me that the marathon is never really over; there are just milestones that I need to appreciate and enjoy. Recovering from a brain injury is a life-long event.

Tom had used going back to work as an indicator of a full recovery, yet as his wife, I dreaded him returning to the profession that nearly killed him in the first place. Once you have a brain injury, a second injury to the head might be the final nail in the coffin. I was terrified, yet for him to not return to work would kill his spirit. I had to make a choice and mentally prepare that I might lose Tom as a result of him returning to work, but I had a 100 percent chance of mentally losing Tom if he never returned to the profession that he loved.

Tom is a computer geek and loves electronics. He had been working on the RMS system, the software system that archived all of the data for the 911 calls in the city, prior to his accident. The fireman he had been working with came to visit Tom at Casa Colina. He was so kind and often brought Tom magazines and asked Tom if he was interested in working with him on a new business model. This gave my mind a little reprieve in case Tom wasn't able to go back as a fireman. There was an alternative for working in the fire service. Thank you God.

Most people predicted that Tom wouldn't live, let alone ever go back to work. I know I struggled with the potential changes in my life. I couldn't imagine what Tom was going through. Since our children had been born, I had opted to work for less money, provide a community service, and in exchange, have flexibility with my work schedule. I prepared myself for a major life change in that I would need to get a job that made a substantial amount of money to support my family. I was angry with myself for not finishing my doctorate. I had about twelve units and a dissertation until I finished my degree. I had resolved that finishing my degree was out of the question and finding a real job would be my priority.

In the meantime, I would work on rehabilitating Tom to his full potential. I honestly didn't know what that meant. I was petrified of him going back to work. Why would I want him to go back to work? Disability wasn't an option in Tom's mind, but to be honest, I did look into it. The world of disability and workmen's compensation was foreign to me. It clearly is a fine-tuned system that one must learn to navigate. It is really designed to prevent people from abusing the system, but when someone is really injured, it is an exhausting maze to navigate. Disability did not seem appealing and I knew that it would be the death of Tom. The only option was to get him back to work.

But the transition back to work was another painful experience in his recovery. The coordination of his return was less than perfect and left me mentally distraught. About six weeks after Tom had his skull replaced, we received a phone call from a fellow firefighter that a memo was displayed on the bulletin board announcing that Tom Barilla was returning to work on Monday, and inviting everyone to join in welcoming him back. The intent of the memo was only love and kindness, but the case management workers failed to tell Tom and me that they had arranged for him to return to work. We had barely recovered from his last surgery and spent every moment of the past six months in therapy or at a doctor's office. We had missed family events, birthdays, vacations, sporting events, school awards ceremonies, and all other social events people attend in a normal life. Now they wanted Tom to return to work and failed to notify us of the date, the conditions, or the circumstances, not to mention the mental preparation for his family. I am not proud of my behavior, but when I was notified of the memo, I called the case manager and practically ripped out her throat. I was so angry, upset, and beyond comprehension that we were not notified and had not developed a plan for Tom's return to work. Did anyone have any idea what our family had just experienced? We had just been through the closest thing to hell I could imagine and on Monday Tom was supposed to return to work. I regret my behavior now, but mentally I was not ready for Tom to go back to work. Please don't misunderstand, we all wanted Tom to return to work, but healing is emotional as well as physical. Our family's emotional healing was completely ignored. Neither Tom nor I, or even the girls, ever received any psychological counseling for this step in the journey. We were offered a few sessions in rehabilitation, but they were far from adequate.

Tom did speak with a neuropsychologist after the lawyers entered his hospital room and showed him pictures of the demolished fire engine, informing him that the accident included a fatality. Tom barely understood that he was in an accident and survived, let alone that there had been a fatality. We were so focused on his physical healing we mistakenly overlooked the emotional healing. Although Tom was medically ready to go back to work, it was just too soon after the accident. I was terrified and had constant nightmares about Tom being injured. Was he really ready to go back to work? You know a broken arm is healed because you can test the range of motion, but how do you test an injured brain? I was told that seizures were a possibility after a brain injury and I was petrified Tom would have one.

This was when my nightmares began. I would wake up in the middle of the night feeling the same emotions I had the day of the accident: the painful realization that I might lose Tom, that the girls might have to grow up without their father, and that I had no control over any of it. It was almost as if someone was sentencing him to his final death. At this point, I realized I needed help. I had taken care of Tom and he was ready to go back to work, but I was dying inside. I had never been fearful of Tom's job in the past. It was what he was called to do and I never questioned anything he did. God would protect him. Now everything was different. Every morning when he walked out the door to go to work I wondered if it would be the last time I ever saw him. Didn't I realize that he had a dangerous job when I married him? What was I thinking? The truth is life is dangerous. Tom could have been driving on the freeway in his Toyota truck and been hit by that bus. It just happened that he was at work that day.

I had given up my life and focused all of my energy on Tom. I was thrilled he was better and so grateful for the final outcome, but something inside me was dying. I couldn't pinpoint my suffering. I had never been one to be depressed, but the realization of where my life was at this point left me feeling as though my life was out of control. I was sleeping until nearly 7:30 every morning and going to bed by 8:00 p.m. This was highly unusual for someone who had gotten up at 4:30 every morning for the past ten years. I had gained thirty pounds and I had infected hair follicles on my legs so bad it looked like I had some type of contagious disease. I was a mess and now they wanted to send Tom back to work. I didn't want my children to leave my sight, I was so afraid. I had nightmares about something happening to my youngest daughter Catie. I had given up the project I was working on as a healthcare consultant. I had no energy left, but I had to smile and be thankful that my husband was alive.

I continued to praise God for his miracle, but it was not easy. Why should I be so thankful that my life was in the gutter? I had been faithful and worked hard my whole life and couldn't understand why was this happening to me. I can remember lying on my bathroom floor crying so hard one morning it felt like I had no fluids left in my body. I finally pulled myself off the floor remembering what my dad use to say: "Dooly-wally — that's what he called me — you can't keep a good man down." I was down, but I couldn't stay there. I believe that this was a pivotal point in my recovery. If I had stayed down at this point my life would never have any peace. Through the grace of God, I pulled myself off the floor that morning and decided to make some phone calls and start putting my life back together. I believe the devil tried to kill me with this incident and I was letting him.

TOM BARILLA:

Daily Bulletin August 4, 2005 — "I have the ability to be reborn into the job I have done before but do it differently — do it better."

TOM BARILLA:

Going back to work was a step toward being normal. It was a relief that I had survived. It was a testament to my wife and my children. I knew that I had to prove myself even though I had returned to work. I still had to prove myself. I was thankful, but honestly there were a few moments that I thought I wasn't able to go back to work, like when I was lying at Casa Colina and regressed in my rehabilitation with paralysis. I felt like I was on a carpet ride that I had no control over. Throughout my rehabilitation, people talked about me in the third person when I was present. Going back to work represented control over my life. But when I went back to work, I realized it wasn't over. There was always another test. People looked at me and wondered if I was really okay. I had to prove myself to everyone. It still wasn't over. If I made a mistake at work it was different. My supervisor could take any incident or mistake and blame it on my brain injury. I was on edge all the time to remember how to get to a call or perform a paramedic procedure. People would always look at me differently.

CATIE BARILLA:

When my dad went back to work I felt happy. I was excited because I knew he could start something new.

REBECCA BARILLA:

I was very proud of my dad, the fact that he had beat the odds. What the doctors said was going to happen to him made him more of a miracle. I liked watching my dad work so hard to go back to work; it was inspirational.

Chapter 16: *Proving Himself at Work. Is He Really Okay?*

Let us not become weary in doing good, for at the proper time we will reap a harvest if we do not give up.
GALATIANS 6:9

OM AND I WERE BOTH RAISED IN VERY AFFLUENT COMMUNITIES in southern California, but neither of our families had money. Both of our parents bought their homes at a time when housing was more affordable. We both came from large families and I was the fourth born of five children, while Tom was the fifth of six children. Needless to say, there was not a lot of money to go around in our families and as a result we both had to go to work at a young age if we wanted to have any additional money. Tom worked at the gas station in his home town and I started working at a real estate company down the street from my high school.

I can't think of a time where either of us has stopped working since this young age. Even while having our children, we alternated our work schedules so one of us could work while the other was home taking care of the kids. Taking time off work to care for Tom was the first time I had been off work for that long since I was fourteen years old. We both have a strong work ethic and take our responsibilities very seriously. It never occurred to either of us that we couldn't work. What happens when you become so severely injured that you can't work? That concept was not even in Tom's consciousness. His sick hours at work had been at their maximum for some time because Tom rarely called in sick. You have a job and a family to support, therefore you go to work.

There were so many questions about Tom going back to work. How could a brain-injured patient go back to being a paramedic/fireman?

Surely this wasn't safe. Had anyone ever done this before? Tom's physician at Casa Colina was his biggest advocate. I don't know if he really believed Tom would go back to work but he did a great job pretending. I brought in paramedic books and fire protocols for his speech therapy. He spent months reviewing protocols and procedures for the fire service while in rehabilitation. Tom was released from therapy in July and began light duty in August. This was only six months after his accident.

JOHN RUPPERT:

Just six months after the accident, Tom went back to work. Back to work, not in the administration office filing paperwork, or answering telephones, but back to work as a fire engineer and paramedic. Back to work, doing what Tom does, fighting fire, operating fire apparatus, and helping people who have no one to turn to.

When Tom went back to work I was not only afraid, but it was the first time in six months that I could stop for a moment and focus on me. I was a mess. I had spent all of my energy taking care of Tom and my children and forgotten about myself. My job of taking care of Tom was over. I felt useless and afraid. I was so grateful Tom went back to work, but it also had wiped out my reason for existence, so I thought. I had a lot of reflection to do at this point. Do you just go back to your old life? My entire life had been blown up and turned upside down. It seemed senseless for me to move forward in my old path. Surely God was not going to waste this tragedy. He must have been preparing me for something. Now what? Just making money didn't seem like an option. I needed to make a difference in our world. I needed to make a difference in our healthcare system. I had witnessed the path to healing. What did God want me to do?

TOM BARILLA:

I was raised in a household where the man provided for his family. I knew not providing for my family was not an option. How was I going to support my children and my wife? Other options seemed dismal. I knew I would go back to work regardless of what any doctor, therapist, or counselor was going to say. I would be going back to work as a firefighter.

Tom and Mike at Quakes Stadium

    To know the fire service, you have to understand that it is a very competitive occupation. I fought hard to become a firefighter. Going back to work, I knew I had to prove to myself that I could do the job as well as I could before the accident; to do anything less would be unacceptable. I knew my limitations and my injuries and I didn't know how they were going to affect the way I did my job. There were only so many things I could simulate in therapy. I wouldn't know until I was in my surroundings and needed to make decisions in a split second. To prove myself worthy, I had to sit down and tell my co-workers that they had to promise me they would tell someone if I wasn't fit for duty. I told them not to lower their level of acceptance because they felt sorry for me. I felt I was putting them in a position that they could end my career. I also felt grateful to the city for giving me the opportunity to prove myself. I believed I could perform the job, but I wouldn't know until I was put in the actual situation. It was very stressful to have to prove myself and ask my co-workers to hold me accountable. I constantly felt that proving myself was something I had to do; I knew I was being watched. When I felt under the spot-

light, I would feel anxious and I would remind myself to just do my job. I finally had to give it up to God and have resolve that if this was what I was meant to do, this was what I would do. I was under a lot of stress with everyone analyzing me pre and post-accident. I knew they were thinking, "Would he have done that before the accident?"

Rarely are two calls the same; I have protocols I needed to follow but most calls cannot be run by protocols alone. I was relieved every day at the end of the shift that I had a successful day. I grew more confident with every shift. When I began making the same types of decisions that I had made before the accident, I knew I was on the right track. Finally people began to comment that they couldn't believe I had a brain injury. I may never really know what I actually lost. I have to work harder now to prove myself. My captain says my memory is better now than before the accident.

It is difficult to explain what I had to experience. A lot of what I went through was that way. To try to make people understand what I was experiencing seemed too difficult. You have to believe you can do it and you have to have people around you believing you can do it. You have to convince yourself first and then surround yourself with people who encourage you.

Chapter 17:
Getting the Family Back to Normal

For we are God's workmanship, created in Christ Jesus to do good works, which God prepared in advance for us to do.
EPHESIANS 2:10

HY DO BAD THINGS HAPPEN TO GOOD PEOPLE? I DON'T KNOW but I have had ample time to ponder this question. Tom's friend asked him that very question and shared a response that made a lot of sense. Bad things happen to good people because it is an opportunity for others to show compassion. In the Bible, Paul pleaded with the Lord three times to take the thorn from his hand, yet God never did. Instead, God told Paul, "My grace is all you need, because my power is perfected in weakness." It is amazing how you can gain strength in the struggles. They are opportunities to be a better person.

There was an elderly gentleman at Casa Colina who had been in an auto accident with his pricy Jaguar and now was unable to walk. He use to say to Tom, "you can't ask why; it doesn't do anyone any good."

I can honestly say I am more compassionate than I was before the accident. I know the power of a kind gesture, flowers, a card, even a smile. Those were the gestures that often kept me going when I thought I couldn't go on. After a horrible tragedy people want to find a sense of normal, some sense of security. I really searched for this after the accident and I can honestly say four years after the accident that will never happen. It is true that Tom went back to work, but I still count the days until he retires so I won't have to worry. The girls are back in school, but I am terrified to let them ride a bus. My professional life was nearly destroyed because of my inability to work after the accident. I went back to work full time as a professor at Loma Linda University School of Public Health and continue to dedicate my life to service but it is safe, secure, and with limited risk. Is that normal? It wasn't for me. I search for a way to get back to the day before the accident. It is like gluing a broken vase back together, yet some pieces are lost and things are never the same. I really don't think of it as being incomplete or inadequate, just very different. People often ask how my children handled the accident; I do believe they are stronger, but they are not the same. Catie still suffers a little anxiety when Tom cannot be reached on his phone while at work. Rebecca still puts people at a distance if she feels emotionally threatened. How do you get back to normal?

I have been told that most marriages don't survive a traumatic brain injury. I can see why. Had our marriage not been strong and we had not had our faith in God, we would have been divorced. When you become the caregiver, pay the bills, make all household decisions, are the sole parent for your children, life can be stressful. Yet then your spouse gets better and you have to reverse gears. I had spent a year making all of the decisions and hoarding every penny for fear of the future. Then Tom was better and going back to work. We defied all odds and we were going to have our lives back to normal. We went through a process of ups and downs. I don't want it to appear as though I wasn't happy, but it was a transition from being the sole provider to making shared decisions again. Over time I became resentful for having to make all of the decisions, but I wouldn't let go of my authority in making those decisions either. I often felt like Tom didn't really have the ability to make the decisions. Although I wanted him to be involved in making decisions, his processing time was delayed at first and I didn't have the patience for him. I resented him for making me make all the decisions. I was tired and I wanted someone to take care of me, but I couldn't let my guard down, because I needed to be alert constantly in case something happened to Tom. I needed him to make decisions, but every time he made a decision I became angry for the choices he made. Basically, I put myself in a self-induced torment. I finally had to receive some counseling to help get through these issues. Tom and I both attended a few sessions of counseling and then I attended on my own. I really needed to let go of those things I had no control over. I began to realize that I couldn't hold my breath for the *what if's* and I needed to let go of being afraid. Tom also needed to build up his confidence and just start making the decisions again. For months Tom would call me before he made any decision. It almost drove me crazy. Tom has since resumed his decision-making, but the journey took several years and was full of torment.

In addition to the mental changes, Tom also experienced significant physical changes. His looks were drastically altered. It is a constant daily reminder of the accident. To this day I struggle to touch his head. His hair covers his scars for the most part, but after his shower when his hair is wet I can see the drastic distortion in his head. The disfiguration isn't what bothers me; it is the pain I feel when I think that he might not be with me today. It has been a process for me to change that thought and remember the miracle God gave our family and begin to feel blessed that he is alive instead of what could have been.

Someone should have told me things will never be the old normal. Life is transformed after a tragedy. You cross a bridge and you can never turn back. Your life is forever changed.

TOM BARILLA:

There is no normal. I don't even know what normal is. My new normal has not yet been defined. It is not over. It will never be normal. Every day is in preparation of the "what ifs." Every time the mail comes or the phone rings I wonder who it is. In fact, what was normal? I struggle to remember what it was like before the accident.

I have always looked at my brain injury like a broken arm. After I heard I had a brain injury, I questioned whether I would act the same before the accident with regards to my response to stress, my attitude, and my personality.

I have come to the realization that it will never be over. Not a day goes by that something doesn't remind me of the accident. I constantly wonder if something is going to happen to my brain. Will I ever be normal?

I empathize with people a lot more now when I respond to an accident. People will say, "You don't know how I feel." I say, "Yes I do." I know when I put that person in the back of the ambulance, the journey has just begun.

After Tom returned to work, it was time for me to put my life back together again as well. I felt like a failure. Who would ever want me to work for them after what had happened in my previous contract? I was experiencing a little fear about re-engaging in health care reform. I had tried to be progressive in a project to improve community health in my previous contract and it fell apart in my absence. I had many friends tell me that it fell apart because it wasn't supposed to happen without me. Others came to the hospital room and wondered if Tom's accident was really an accident and questioned if someone hurt Tom in an attempt to stop my work in health care. I didn't believe that was the case, but the question did haunt me and placed enough fear in me to change the focus of my efforts. Going back to what I had started before the accident seemed almost impossible. I felt as though my life was spinning out of control and had been broken into a million little pieces and I only had few pieces left. I was left all alone to put the rest of my life back together.

I was about three-fourths through a doctoral program at Loma Linda University, but I didn't see how I could possibly have any brain matter left after what I had experienced. I contemplated staying home and taking care of my husband and my girls. After all, I could become an overbearing mother and wife and protect them from all the evils in the world. I can honestly say this was a point in my life that I felt closer to a nervous breakdown than any other time. I felt as though I was assessing damage after someone purposely exploded a bomb on my project. I felt personally responsible for the damage it did to people and knew that if I didn't face the damage right in the face I would never venture out again on an exciting new project to try and improve health care. I would admit defeat and never help anyone again. I knew that we were about to embark upon litigation and my life was in pieces After what I had experienced, I spent some time reflecting what God wanted me to do and He led me to Loma Linda University. I knew I wasn't the same; I was changed forever and I couldn't go back to what I was doing. I had something to give back and I needed to make sense of what I had just experienced.

I started taking classes in September at Loma Linda to try and finish up my doctorate and began making appointments to rebuild my career. Everything seemed so irrelevant, people would complain about the most mundane issues in life. I would think to myself, how lucky you are to have such issues to deal with, let me tell you about a real problem. I found myself unable to connect with people. I didn't want to feel uncompassionate; on the contrary, I wanted to be more compassionate, but with people with real problems. My litmus test for stress had been altered forever. I was searching for my path but I was very confused. I finally came to the realization that I needed help. I also needed time to heal. I hadn't given myself any room to process what I had been through. I knew I needed time, but I was so anxious and I wanted God to reveal His plans for me NOW.

I thank God that He knows me so well. Loma Linda University offered me a job on the faculty in the Health Policy and Management Department. It was a perfect opportunity for me to give back and work in a safe environment. I could teach health care administration and policy courses standing on my head with my hands tied behind my back. I had spent the majority of my career in health care, therefore teaching health policy seemed like a logical choice. I also knew I needed some flexibility and something to keep my mind occupied through the litigation. I honestly thought it would be a safe place to take a break and move on when my nightmare was over and when I finished my degree. Little did I know that God wanted me there and that I would love it as much as I do. I never really thought about the fact that Loma Linda University was one of the major Christian Health Science Universities in the USA. It was a perfect place for me to work in health policy, while continuing my exploration of healing through body, mind, and spirit. It was also a place where people could openly pray for me through my ordeal. I was very fortunate to have amazing co-workers, partners, and students at Loma Linda. They helped me heal, grow, and find purpose in my tragedy. I believe God used my tragedy to lead me to where I was suppose to be.

The first time we were able to get away after Tom's accident, we visited the Sequoia National Forest. My family has owned land just outside the national park since the 1940s and I spent many summers there camping and hiking. I have always loved the peace and tranquility of these beautiful mountains. Tom didn't have the stamina yet to camp, so we stayed in a nearby hotel and spent the day visiting the park and beautiful sequoia trees. As we walked through the park, I spotted so many large trees that had been either struck by lightning or had been burned in the middle. It was fascinating to see the trees that had grown for years and obviously experienced some type of tragedy, been scarred, yet continued to grow and sprout new limbs. I took a picture of the tree and told Tom that it resembled our life. We had grown for years, healthy and productive and a tragedy hit our life scarring it forever, but there was a promise of new beginnings if we persevered. I was struck how the tree was stronger and more beautiful on the other side of the burns. I told Tom that would be us some day. We would be stronger on the other side of this tragedy.

Chapter 18: *The Guilt*

*Even though my illness was a trial to you, you did not treat
me with contempt or scorn. Instead, you welcomed me as if I
were an angel of God, as if I were Christ Jesus himself.*
GALATIANS 4:14

WHEN TOM CAME HOME FROM CASA COLINA FOR THE FIRST
time and was greeted by local fire engines and police cars in
our driveway, I was completely unaware of the terror this
scene would bring to our neighbors. They had heard about Tom's accident from the newspapers and television, but they knew very little about
his condition. The barrage of emergency personnel at our home put them
a little on edge.

As I was walking some of the firefighters out of the house, I saw my
neighbors bringing food to another house. They stopped me on the sidewalk and asked if everything was alright with Tom. I explained that the
firefighters and police officers were just there to welcome Tom home. One
of my neighbors commented that a lot of tragedy had struck their street in
the past several months and asked if I had heard about Alan. I had been
so self-absorbed in my own tragedy I hadn't heard anything. One of our
neighbors had been killed in a motorcycle accident. I stood in the street
paralyzed. I didn't know what was wrong. Alan and Lisa were our neighbors, about the same age as Tom and I, with young children. Lisa and her
husband had stopped by our house with a card and a grocery gift card
two weeks ago consoling me. This news was more than I could bear. It
hit me like a rock. My emotions became uncontrollable; the tears welled
up in my eyes and I began to cry uncontrollably. I had rejoiced that Tom
was alive and had come home from the hospital against all odds, while
Lisa mourned for her dead husband just two doors down. As I stood on
my sidewalk stunned, Alan's older son walked out of the house. I hugged
him and told him I was so sorry and we both stood in the street and cried.

Why had my husband lived and hers had died? How could I celebrate my miracle now? This did not make sense to me. I couldn't bear the guilt. I immediately went home and wrote a sympathy card, along with the money they had given to me two weeks ago. To this day, I struggle with that paradigm. I see a widow raising three small children by herself and it breaks my heart. Why is that not me? I often ask God what I am to do for her. I am confident he will reveal it to me.

Remembering the angel bracelet our associate pastor's wife had given me at the hospital while Tom was still in a coma, and the miracle I had received, I was clearly led to give Lisa that bracelet. Although her husband had died, she still needed to be reminded of God's love. Sometimes miracles don't come in the form we imagine them, but they do come.

Several months later, while getting a pedicure at the nail shop down the street, I ran into my next door neighbor Kathy. I greeted her in the usual manner, but noticed something was not right with her behavior. She eventually realized I hadn't heard the news — that her husband had developed an infection from knee surgery last week and had died. She was getting her nails done for the funeral.

Three houses in a row on our street: mine, Kathy's, and Lisa's. Tom had nearly been killed in March, Lisa's husband died in April, and Kathy's in June. What was that saying about things coming in three's? Again I pondered why Tom lived. I sat in the nail shop speechless. Why was God putting all of this in my life? I felt guilty that Tom lived. It was a raw emotion. I am confident that both of my neighbors were good people, they deserved a miracle, too. Why were their husbands taken and not mine?

Asking why is not a healthy state. I have learned that you can only ask "What am I to learn from this?" What was I to do for my neighbors? Jim Reeves wrote a book titled, *God Never Wastes a Hurt*. I read it while Tom was in rehabilitation and it appeared it was time to put the principles I learned into action. The book helped me discover how God can help us, 1) find opportunity and healing in the valleys of life, 2) detect false guilt that steals our freedom and joy, 3) develop a lifestyle of forgiveness, 4) see tragedy from Heaven's perspective, and 5) reach out to others with power and authority.

This was also the first time I realized I needed to write a book to help others heal. There were very few books on traumatic brain injuries written for families. I had access to medical libraries to research information on brain injuries, but that information was never comforting, only discouraging. I found comfort in reading how others had persevered. This was the beginning of my journey to reach out to others with power and authority. I had to make the decision to be a victim or be victorious.

Tom Barilla:

People would say to me, "God must have a plan for your life; He must not have been finished with you." Although I know this must have been words of encouragement, I would think to myself that God has a plan for ALL of us. Why do you need a bus accident to realize that? God has a plan for you, too; why wait for a tragedy to realize that? Go out and fulfill your purpose now!

Chapter 19:
Post-Traumatic Stress Disorder

*'For I know the plans I have for you,' declares
the LORD, 'plans to prosper you and not to
harm you, plans to give you hope and a future.'*
JEREMIAH 29:11

LIFE WAS BACK TO NORMAL. I COULD TAKE MY DAUGHTERS TO a movie on a Sunday afternoon. The girls and I, along with two of their friends, had just enjoyed a Sunday matinee without the worries we had carried for so many months. Tom was back to work, and all was well with the world.

Or so I thought. Tom had been put back together, literally piece by piece. I had counted the days until his skull was put back in, then his teeth, then back to work, then life would be back to the day before the accident. Wrong. As we walked out of the theatre that day, my daughters needed to use the restroom, so I waited outside the door and saw a group of brain-injury patients wearing the same helmet Tom wore while his skull was removed. I watched a middle-aged man drool and struggle to walk. It was then that it hit me. The levy broke and the emotions I had been suppressing began to flood my body. I couldn't breathe and I needed to get out of the theatre. I drove home and cried for hours on the floor in my bedroom. I didn't understand what was wrong. Why was this hitting me now? I had dealt with my tragedy and life had moved on. Was my reaction a delayed response to the trauma I had just experienced?

I have never been one to be depressed. I have always seen the glass half full, regardless of my circumstances. I had experienced tragedy before in my life and I was always able to make the best of my situations. I had great coping skills. So why were my emotions out of control now? People would stop me on the streets and ask me about Tom and I would smile and say,

"He is back to work without any restrictions." They would always respond positively, yet I couldn't understand why I felt so empty and alone. I had just been given one of the greatest miracles of my life: I had my husband, he was back to work, and the end result was more than I ever could have asked for. Was I just ungrateful? Did I miss the attention I had received when Tom was sick? I did not expect a delayed response to this trauma. I was struggling accepting normal life. I was having serious memory problems and difficulty concentrating. I was irritable and the nightmares were coming in full force.

I was talking on the phone with a friend one day and she suggested that I may be experiencing post-traumatic stress disorder (PTSD). I thought she might be misguided in her suggestion; post-traumatic stress disorder was something that veterans of war experienced, not the wife of a traumatic brain injury patient. I began to research the symptoms and was surprised to find that I was experiencing some of them.

Post-traumatic stress disorder develops after a terrifying ordeal that involves physical harm or the threat of physical harm. The person who develops PTSD may have been the one who was harmed, or the person may have witnessed the harm happen to a loved one, or even a stranger. The signs and symptoms of post-traumatic stress disorder didn't begin for me until a year after the accident.

Although I didn't experience all of the following symptoms, I found knowing the range of what could occur very helpful. Post-traumatic stress disorder symptoms may include:

- Flashbacks or reliving the traumatic event for minutes or even days at a time
- Shame or guilt
- Upsetting dreams about the traumatic event
- Trying to avoid thinking or talking about the traumatic event
- Feeling emotionally numb
- Irritability or anger
- Poor relationships
- Self-destructive behavior, such as drinking too much
- Hopelessness about the future
- Trouble sleeping
- Memory problems
- Trouble concentrating

- Being easily startled or frightened
- Not enjoying activities once enjoyed
- Hearing or seeing things that aren't there

After coming to the conclusion that I might be experiencing some difficulties, I decided to make an appointment with my doctor for a physical examination. At my appointment the doctor assessed the normal health measures: my weight, blood pressure, pulse, and reflexes. Despite a little weight gain, everything seemed fine. I then began to tell her about Tom's accident and what I had experienced over the past year. As I shared with her my experience, I began to cry. She stated that many people find a low dose of antidepressants helpful in these situations. I wanted to scream. Society has a quick fix for everything and wants to suppress normal rational feelings. Didn't she understand that people need time to heal, that some painful emotions are a part of the healing process? Not that antidepressants aren't helpful for some people, but wouldn't it be stranger if I wasn't mourning my situation? I declined and told her I limit my aspirin intake, let alone a foreign drug that may have adverse side effects. I would prefer to deal with my memory problems, irritability, and sleeping troubles via other methods. I began to exercise, write, and strategize how I could help others.

Post-traumatic stress disorder symptoms can come and go. More symptoms appear during times of higher stress or when there are symbolic reminders of the trauma. Sure enough, my symptoms returned when my stress levels were higher. The first time my daughter took a bus to San Francisco for a school trip I didn't sleep for three days. I was afraid to go to sleep, fearful that the nightmares would return and this time they would include my daughter Rebecca. I wouldn't have the assurance of checking her room to ensure her safety, so sleepless nights were a better option. I had already been waking up at two a.m. every night with an absolute fear that something was wrong, but when my stress levels were higher those moments of waking up for an hour or so became all-night rituals of not sleeping. I began reading my Bible in the middle of the night rather than lying there and waking up Tom to make sure he was okay.

I would relive the traumatic event numerous times or I would experience upsetting memories. There were reminders everywhere I went. I wasn't even there the morning the bus hit the fire engine, but after the numerous pictures, newspaper articles, court cases, and videos, the scene was etched in my brain. When I would hear a car backfire or a loud bang I would picture the fire engine being hit by the bus. When I would see or hear about an injury in the media, I would relive the horror and fear of our family's tragedy.

I found I was losing interest in things I used to enjoy. I was having trouble feeling affectionate and I became very irritable at times, especially when Tom didn't remember something. Both Tom and I would avoid situations that reminded us of the original incident. Tom stopped getting the mail, because there was usually a letter from a lawyer discussing the case, which reminded him daily of the accident. The anniversaries of the incident became very difficult. After the first year, we decided to get together with friends and family on March 15th and celebrate the blessings we had been given rather than focus on the negative. I would repeatedly relive the accident in my thoughts during the day and in nightmares when I slept. I was experiencing flashbacks of Tom being in a coma and smelling the scent of his hospital room. Often I would lose touch with reality and forget that Tom was really okay. I couldn't believe this was happening to me. I thought I had handled everything so well. Why was this happening now?

After surviving a traumatic event, it is difficult to stop thinking about what's happened. Fear, anxiety, anger, depression, guilt — were all too common. Although I didn't want to talk about it to anyone or couldn't bear reliving the accident over and over again during litigation, getting support and asking for help allowed me to recover. My mom moved in with us to help with our daily challenges. I also decided I needed to get help from a counselor affiliated with our church. I honestly felt as though I had a serious deficit in relying on my friends and family. They had given so much already, how could I possibly lean on anyone more than I already had? Shouldn't I be giving back, not continuing to drain my friends and family? They had to be sick of hearing about my troubles; I know I was sick of them myself. I didn't even know how to articulate what was happening to me; how could I talk about it to someone else?

A good friend suggested that we start walking on the weekends. She knew I was concerned about my weight gain and thought it was a supportive suggestion. It was a blessing to have some time each week to just talk about my feelings without judgment or having someone trying to fix my problems. She only listened and asked clarifying questions. At the time this book was written, we were still walking. These walks were an important part of my healing process.

It did help to see our counselor, but I also looked at actions I could take to help myself. I found these suggestions from the Mayo Clinic website and really used them to help me cope.

- Take care of yourself. Get enough rest, eat a balanced diet, exercise, and take time to relax. Avoid caffeine and nicotine, which can worsen anxiety.
- Don't self-medicate. Turning to alcohol or drugs to numb your feelings isn't healthy, even though it may be a tempting way to cope. It can lead to more problems down the road and prevent real healing.
- Break the cycle. When you feel anxious, take a brisk walk or delve into a hobby to refocus.
- Talk to someone. Stay connected with supportive and caring family, friends, faith leaders, or others. You don't have to talk about what happened if you don't want to. Just sharing time together with loved ones can offer healing and comfort.
- Consider a support group. Many communities have support groups geared for specific situations. Ask your health care professional for help finding one, look in your local phone book, or contact your community's social services system.
- Make a resolution. For many people, living through a traumatic event becomes a turning point to make positive changes in their lives and grow emotionally and psychologically.

As a part of my healing process I have made a decision to address the current penalties for not yielding to emergency vehicles and to reach out to other brain injury patients.

My children were also experiencing delayed stress from the accident that I hadn't realized until I became aware of my own denial. I am on the board of our community hospital and one evening I received a call about someone who had received a brain injury and thought I might be able to help the family cope. I spent an hour on the telephone consoling the family and friends of the family, not realizing my nine-year-old daughter at the time was absolutely petrified. She didn't know who I was talking about and worried it may have pertained to her father. I will never forget the look on her face that evening. I was far more cognizant of my words around my children after that incident. Catie observes everything and I should have known better. I continue to learn how the accident impacted my children. The impact of trauma manifests so differently in each individual. If things are not right with your behavior, take some time to reflect and understand that you may be processing very painful emotions.

I still wake up some nights in a panic that won't go away. It used to happen quite often, but now only occurs once in a while. I wake up with the same feeling I had the first night after the accident. One of absolute terror and that Tom is not there. I can't breathe and just want it to be morning. The nightmares were the worst, but those stopped about three years after the accident. I would relive the scene in the hospital over and over in my head, but in my nightmares the outcome wasn't good.

Our bodies have an amazing ability to protect ourselves through tragedy and often dealing with the emotional trauma is delayed until we are healthy enough to handle it. Don't be fooled that the healing is over once the physical body is restored. Most traumatic injuries come with an emotional healing process that may not manifest until years later. Be prepared and use the techniques mentioned in this chapter; they really work. Most of all, avoid self-medicating; I guarantee it will only prevent the emotional healing from taking place.

Chapter 20: *Litigation*

Do not exploit the poor because they are poor and do not crush the needy in court, for the Lord will take up their case and will plunder those who plunder them.
PROVERBS 22:22–23

*T*HE UNITED STATES HAS BECOME SUCH A LITIGIOUS SOCIETY. WHY can't an accident just be an accident? Does someone always have to pay? I remember the first time someone mentioned the idea of litigation while Tom was still in a coma; I was shocked. Unfortunately they were right. An attorney visited me in the waiting room of Arrowhead Regional Medical Center, and I was told that I should be proactive and protect Tom. I couldn't believe my ears. Wasn't almost taking his life enough?

JOEL CASCADDEN:

Life is a series of tests, small and large, of tremendous consequence and minor. But all are important in some way, just like a test at school that determines knowledge, intelligence, and one's ability to make progress — or not.

Life is also a series of disappointments, again both small and large, and of varying consequence.

And while we journey through life being tested and being disappointed, we get to choose. We choose to be a victim or not. While this is a rather simple choice, many, maybe most, choose to be the victim. I suppose this occurs because it is easy. It is easy to blame others, difficult to accept responsibility for one's self and situation. We watch this happening everyday on TV, at work, on the playground and in our own neighborhoods. The winners are the lawyers.

With all due respect to our attorneys, Joel is right. Litigation does not create justice or closure; it just produces more stress and a lot of money for lawyers. Often lawyers become immune to the trauma that most people face during litigation. We had numerous lawyers involved in this case; some were there to defend the wronged and many were there to take advantage of the situation.

We were blessed with attorneys who wanted to fight for the good in the world, including the best defense attorney I had ever met, Steve Rothans. Tom and Joel loved Steve; he was a fighter, but a thoughtful, calm, and patient fighter. He left nothing unaccounted for. He knew more about this case than anyone. I was so grateful he was on our side. He always reminded Tom and me never to be afraid in any of our depositions, but just to tell the truth. That was easy and it felt good to have a lawyer with integrity. I loved that about Steve. We also had a wonderful personal injury attorney, Dave Berglund. Dave is a Christian and not afraid to praise God in public. Dave had the reputation as the most honest attorney in the business. He would always tell the truth. We had a team that anyone would envy. If lawyers had to make any money from this case, I was glad it would be Dave and Steve. They deserved every penny.

I was fooled into believing that litigation would bring closure. If anything, it produced more pain. I had refrained from talking about many of the details of the accident over the past three years, because we were advised not to talk about the pending litigation with anyone. That was really a shame, because I believe that talking about it, rather than holding everything inside, might have brought the closure I had been searching for.

We had a litigation nightmare on our hands. Everyone was suing everyone. There were suits against the bus company, the bus driver, the city of Upland, and Tom. Everyone was a plaintiff and a defendant. For four years following the accident we received letters from lawyers about every week. We hated to get the mail.

Three years, nine months, and two days after the accident, we finally had a trial date. We had been through a living hell and now it was public and in front of the world. I felt numb at this point and not much could have fazed me. I was a much different person than I was on March 14, 2005. My department chair often comments that he is amazed at how things that he thinks should impact me don't seem to bother me, and things that seem irrelevant to him upset me so much. His comments represent my shift in priorities; I have a new litmus test for stress. I become very upset with things that hurt people and could care less about the mundane drama in the workplace. I know what matters at the end of the day. I have been to the edge and seen the other side. People, relationships, and integrity matter; everything else is just a distraction.

I was scared for the trial. I was afraid that someone was going to say that Tom did something wrong. The bus company's lawyers wanted him to be the bad guy. They didn't care about Tom, just how much money they could get if they claimed he was at fault. The thought that our tragedy was profiting so many lawyers made me sick. The longer they prolonged our pain the more money they made.

Webster's dictionary defines closure as "an often comforting or satisfying sense of finality." The problem with closure with a traumatic brain injury is that you don't know when it is over. What is the sense of finality? Five years after the accident? When Tom doesn't have any complications? When he retires from work? When he dies? When I stop crying every time I think about the accident? When the nightmares go away? When? I often wish I could wrap it all up in a box and tie it with a bow and then it would all be over, but the reality is our journey may never be over. Litigation was just another hurdle.

Chapter 21: *The Accident Report*

*For we know the one who said, 'Vengeance belongs to me;
I will pay them back,' and again, 'The Lord will judge his people.'*
HEBREWS 10:30

DAILY BULLETIN

REPORT: FIREFIGHTER AT FAULT IN CRASH WITH TOUR BUS
UPLAND OFFICIALS BLAST RESULTS OF INVESTIGATION INTO FATAL CRASH
By Edward Barrera, Staff Writer
Article Launched: 04/06/2006 12:00:00 a.m. PDT

UPLAND — State investigators blame an Upland firefighter for causing a crash last year on the 10 Freeway that killed one man and injured dozens.

According to a California Highway Patrol report released Wednesday, the firetruck driven by engineer Tom Barilla made an unsafe lane change into the carpool lane on March 15, 2005, cut in front of a casino tour bus and was the "proximate cause of this collision."

Upland firefighters were responding to an early morning emergency near the Fourth Street exit when their truck collided with the tour bus, killing a seventy-five-year-old Rosemead man, severely injuring Barilla, and sending more than fifty others to nearby hospitals.

While Barilla, who doesn't remember the day of the accident, said he couldn't comment Wednesday because he hadn't read the report, Upland officials blasted the review.

"We have concluded that the report mistakenly and incorrectly reached a conclusion that the city's fire unit approaching the accident did not conform to the rules of the road," City Attorney William Curley said.

"The CHP *interpreted the evidence available to it well after the fact, and substituted its opinion for that of the veteran firefighter who was at the wheel."*

Curley said Barilla's stellar fourteen-year record, as well as the condition of the tour bus, owned by H & C Paradise Tour Inc., and the actions of the bus's driver led the city to conclude the fault of the crash lies with the bus and its driver, Nam Jae Chung.

A CHP *official could not be reached for comment.*

A lawyer for the tour bus company said she had not yet read the nearly 230-page document.

"I withhold making a comment until I have an opportunity to review the report," Kara Pape said.

Tom Dempsey, lawyer for the family of the Rosemead man killed, Kau Leung, also said he hadn't read the report and couldn't comment. The Leung family has filed a lawsuit, along with fifteen other lawsuits filed against Barilla, the city, and the tour bus company.

The vehicles collided on the eastbound side of the freeway about 7:30 a.m. as the Upland fire unit was responding to a minor car accident on the westbound carpool lane.

Barilla, along with Captain Joel Cascadden and firefighter-paramedic John Rupert, entered the 10 from Euclid Avenue, according to the CHP *report. After locating the car accident, Cascadden and Barilla decided to cross the eastbound lanes and stop in the carpool lane to assist, the report indicated.*

Barilla activated all the emergency lighting equipment but did not turn on the siren, the report said. Vehicles began to slow and then stop, as the truck slowly began to drive across the eastbound lanes, it said.

Several witnesses said that Barilla even had his hand out of the left window, signaling traffic to remain stopped. One eyewitness said the truck stopped prior to entering the carpool lane.

The driver of the tour bus, Chung, said he saw the firetruck before the accident but never saw the emergency lights, according to the report. Eyewitnesses said they observed the lights, which was why they slowed down.

Investigators said state law requires vehicles to exit the carpool lane when an emergency vehicle displaying red lights or sirens approaches the lane. But emergency vehicles can only enter the lane when there is no "immediate hazard," investigators said.

The report said it was possible that Chung did not see the emergency lights flashing and that it was up to Barilla to make sure he entered the carpool lane with reasonable safety.

Though investigators concluded that the tour bus was driving at 73 mph, had brake deficiencies, and a worn tire, they said the responsibility was Barilla's to make sure no vehicles were coming. The firetruck did not give the tour bus a reasonable amount of time to respond, investigators said.

Cascadden, who rode with Barilla the day of the crash and scanned the CHP report, was livid with the investigators' conclusion.

"I find their discovery, their report, and their opinion deplorable," he said, before declining further comment.

John Fowler, president of the Upland firefighter union, was floored when he heard the news.

"I'm in shock and disbelief because I know the type of driver Tom is and the training he has had," Fowler said. "I have a hard time believing they took everything into account."

Investigators also recommended the report be forwarded to the San Bernardino County District Attorney's Office, which Upland's city attorney said was a routine recommendation rather than any belief that there were criminal violations involved.

THE CRASH

Upland fire engineer Tom Barilla, Captain Joel Cascadden, and firefighter-paramedic John Ruppert were responding March 15 to a minor car accident. As their firetruck merged into the carpool lane, it collided with a casino tour bus.

THE OUTCOME

A seventy-five-year-old Rosemead resident was killed, and Barilla was ejected from his cab and suffered severe head trauma. Dozens sustained injuries and were transported to nearby hospitals.

Barilla, who has no memory of the events, was in intensive care at Arrowhead Regional Medical Center in Colton for about two weeks. He was transferred to Casa Colina Rehabilitation Center in Pomona. Barilla had both inpatient and outpatient therapy for about fifteen weeks.

The Upland firefighter returned to light duty in September and full duty by October.

THE LITIGATION

In total, since the accident, sixteen lawsuits have been filed. While lawsuits can be filed against the city up to one year after an incident, additional litigation can still be filed against the tour bus company, H & C Paradise Tour, Inc.

WHEN TOM WAS STILL IN A COMA, THE CHP WANTED TO TALK to both Joel and John, the other two firefighters on the engine the day of the accident. Apparently there was a delay in this exchange, which made the head of the Major Accident Investigation Team (MAIT) angry. He stated that if his team could not talk to Joel and John, the team would file manslaughter charges against Tom. This was not only a verbal threat, but was communicated in an email, which was then sent to this individual's supervisor. He was removed from the case. The frustration that the removal caused the remaining team played out in the weeks that followed and to me explained their misguided conclusions.

MAIT is a mystery to me. A CHP officer was instrumental in saving Tom's life the morning of the accident, and for that I am extremely grateful. But I cannot understand their motivation in trying to find fault with Tom, and for that I am extremely hurt and upset. I am more amazed, though, at the forgiving nature of my husband. He would only comment that the guys in the field are admirable. Never faulting the whole for the misguided deeds of a few. My husband truly is a man of integrity.

I am also very grateful for the star witness in the case. She was in the first car of the first lane on the freeway that day of the accident. She was the best witness at the scene, yet no one took her statement. I thank God for her persistence in telling her story. She was a true hero. Having absolutely no stake in the matter and only wanting to see the truth, she went out of her way to give her statement..

TAKEN FROM THE DEPOSITION OF THE EYE WITNESS ON THE FREEWAY THE MORNING OF THE ACCIDENT:

When I arrived at work I asked how the fireman was, and my co-worker wondered how I knew about it. I told her I was there. She commented that they didn't have any witnesses, and asked if she could call someone to contact me. A California Highway Patrolman called and asked if anyone questioned me during that time. I told him no. Then he came to my work and wanted to see if there was any damage to my car. Why he wanted to know that I didn't know, but from the phone interview he assumed I wanted to press charges for damage to my car. Then he said something about, "You don't have any damage to your car."

I said, "No, I don't."

He said, "Well, I thought you wanted to make a claim on your vehicle getting hit."

I said, "No, not at all. That was the last thing on my mind."

Then he made a comment that ever since 9/11, they like firemen more than policemen and they are always trying to help them.

He said he just wanted to be clear about everything that had happened. But he didn't ask me any questions and said that I had got him in trouble, because I had made a statement that no one asked me any questions during the time of or after the accident.

He said they didn't ask me any questions, because they rushed me off the freeway.

In the report, the CHP faulted Tom and the city of Upland for faulty lighting and an unsafe lane change. The claim that the lights were faulty was explored because the bus driver claimed he did not see the emergency lights. The lighting became an important issue because if the lighting was faulty, then it would remove the exemptions of an emergency vehicle. When the issue of the lighting was challenged by other industry professionals, the CHP backed off the fact that the lights on the fire engine may have been a contributor If they wanted to hold claim to their original statements of faulty lighting, then every fire engine in America would be out of compliance and we would have some real problems.

DEPOSITION OF THE CHP MAIT TEAM:

Question: *If I may ask you to turn your attention to page 204 of the MAIT report and ask you to read very carefully for us into the record the provisions of California Vehicle Code 21655.8 Subsection B only.*

Witness: *"Upon the approach of an authorized emergency vehicle displaying a red light or siren, as specified in Section 21806, a person driving a vehicle in an exclusive or preferential lane shall exit that lane immediately upon determining that the exit can be accomplished with reasonable safety."*

FURTHER TESTIMONY:

Witness: *The primary collision factor was 22107 of the California Vehicle Code and it states, "A vehicle shall not move left to right on a highway until reasonably safe to do so." I mean there's more to that section actually than that specifically, and that violation was committed by engineer Barilla.*

FURTHER TESTIMONY:

Question: *Would you agree that the ultimate objective of the MAIT team was the utilization of identified causation factors in order to prevent collisions of similar nature from recurring?*

Answer: *That's part of it yes.*

Question: *In your 226-page investigative report, you made certain conclusions with respect to the inadequacies of the emergency lighting on the fire engine. Is that true?*

Answer: *I don't know that they were referenced as inadequacies. They were violations of specific sections of the Government Code.*

Question: *Given your findings or conclusions of such violations, did you in your role make any recommendations to anyone at the CHP that in order to protect the motoring public, the manufacturer of the lighting system on the fire engine should be notified about these violations?*

Answer: *No I did not do that, no.*

Question: *What happens when a CHP officer stops a Chinese-American or Korean-American on a freeway and there's a language barrier? What happens?*

Answer: *Unfortunately or fortunately, depending on what side you're on, they get let go. We can't communicate with the multiple dialects in this community we live in.*

Question: *You don't issue them a citation?*

Answer: *Not if you can't communicate with them, you don't.*

Counsel: *Got to remember that one.*

The majority of the passengers on the bus did not speak English and as a result were not questioned. The bus driver also was not proficient in English, but fortunately they found a way to interview him.

Question: *After the MAIT team completed their investigation into this accident, you made some recommendations to the DA's office. Is that correct?*

Answer: *We presented the case to the District Attorney's office. I wouldn't ever say we recommended the case. We had a meeting with two representatives of the District Attorney's office.*

Question: *And what was the response of the DA's office during the meeting?*

Answer: *Actually, I was really kind of taken aback. We presented the completed report and they didn't even look at it and said they would not file charges against a firefighter responding to an emergency call. They would not prosecute him. I made the comment that you know it would be different if it was a Highway Patrol Officer. He said, "Absolutely. He's a fireman and we cannot get a prosecution or conviction for a fireman doing his job, responding to an emergency call." Period. And I was taken aback. He never even looked at it. Their opinion was the report lacked corpus delecti, which I thought was really kind of a slap in our face. I don't think they took an objective approach in reviewing it. That's based on the way we were treated in our initial presentation.*

I was told by our defense attorney that the CHP had gone to the district attorney to file manslaughter charges against Tom for the accident; I was horrified. Thank God the district attorney had enough sense not to pursue. This apparently didn't make the CHP very happy. The behavior of the CHP made me feel as though they literally took the bus that hit Tom, put it in reverse, and backed over our family. We had survived the physical injuries; now the CHP was determined to kill us emotionally. For weeks after the accident report was released I would wake up in the middle of the night with excruciating pain. The only remedy that would bring me comfort was continuous prayer. There was not enough aspirin to take away the pain of betrayal; only God was capable of healing my soul.

According to the CHP report, the bus was approximately a football field away when Tom entered the High Occupancy Vehicle lane. A rational person would assume the bus would slow down and not maintain a speed of 78 miles per hour. The black box on the bus indicated that the brakes were not applied until a few seconds before impact; in fact, the speed was increased before the brakes were applied. That would coincide with the statement from one of passengers that indicated the bus driver said, "We need to get around this fire engine or we will be stuck here all day."

I really tried to understand the dynamics of the CHP. They should have been working together with firefighters to prevent future accidents from careless drivers not yielding to emergency vehicles. All emergency vehicles are impacted by drivers not yielding, not just fire engines and paramedics; in fact, I saw more CHP officers than firefighters at Casa Colina learning to walk and talk again.

The mission statement and organizational goals of the CHP are to:

- Prevent loss of life, and property damage
- Maximize service to the public and assistance to allied agencies
- Manage traffic and emergency incidents
- Protect public and state assets
- Improve departmental deficiency

I believed that the CHP failed in their duties by not citing the bus driver. I also truly believed that Tom's accident and the results of the trial would set precedent on yielding to emergency vehicles. To let this bus driver off the hook or to have Tom at fault would put all emergency personnel at greater risk. It should be more of an offense not to yield. I plan one day to advocate for harsher penalties towards those who do not yield to emergency vehicles, but I am waiting for the right platform. I am looking forward to the opportunity to constructively utilize my policy expertise and years of pain and torment to move forward legislation that protects our first responders while taveling to the scene of an accident. And yes, the CHP can be assured I will fight for them as well, because it is the right thing to do. Some people still hold that as a value. The Bible teaches us to repay evil with kindness and I will take that to heart. I will have to let those CHP officers stand before God and explain their behavior.

During my deposition, I was asked if I was angry. I really had to think about that. Was I angry? I guess I was angry that this accident turned my life upside down. But in all honesty, I am haunted by the actions of the CHP. What would motivate anyone to want to torment Tom and his family? Why would anyone try to develop a case against a firefighter who was responding to a call? Tom almost lost his life and will suffer from his injuries for the rest of his life. Tom was serving his community that day and the bus didn't yield to an emergency vehicle. That is the bottom line.

Chapter 22: *Reaching Out to Other Brain Injury Patients*

And we know that in all things God works for the good of those who love him, who have been called according to his purpose.
ROMANS 8:28

RECEIVED A CALL ON THE 5TH OF JANUARY IN 2007 FROM THE MAYOR of Ontario, Paul Leon, concerned about one of their firemen who had suffered a head injury and had experienced a craniectomy. The mayor had comforted me two years earlier and thought we might be able to bring comfort to this family. The fireman had been airlifted to Arrowhead Regional Medical Center. Tom and I happened to be on one of our annual camping trips with several other firemen in Carlsbad, California. The call took a significant toll on me. I couldn't stop thinking about the family and the fear they had to be experiencing. When Tom was injured, I used to wonder if we would ever do anything normal again. Now we were actually doing something normal and a fellow firefighter and his family were in our old shoes. It was unbelievable.

The network of fireman is pretty powerful. Not long after I received the call from the mayor, a fellow Ontario firefighter called Mike, Tom's brother, asking about Tom's whereabouts and if we would be willing to talk to the family of the injured firefighter. Both Tom and I thought we would give them our right arm if they needed it. You cannot know the pain this family was feeling unless you have been there yourself. Mike gave the firefighter our cell phone numbers and told them to call anytime.

We returned the next day and I could not stop thinking about the family. I left a message on the wife's cell phone. She never returned my call and I knew it was because she was completely overwhelmed. I couldn't stop thinking about her and decided that Tom and I needed to visit the hospital, so Tom and I drove out to Arrowhead Regional Medical Center.

Every time I walk into that hospital, I relive the pain of March 15, 2005. Tom didn't experience the same feelings, as he had no memory of his stay there. The difference was that this time I was walking into the hospital with Tom by my side.

We went up to the second floor, again the same floor Tom had been on, and walked into the waiting room outside the ICU where family and friends were gathered. And yes, it was the same waiting room that I had lived in for two weeks immediately following Tom's accident. But it was different this time. The feelings were different; I wasn't the victim; No one knew who I was.

This was my time to give back a portion of what I had received. I introduced myself to the wife of the firefighter. When she realized who we were, her face lit up and she started asking a million questions. What should I expect? Will he be normal again? Will we ever be intimate again? Is Tom really okay? The beauty of this situation was that Tom was with me. He sat next to me and answered her questions as well. She asked if she could touch Tom's scar. She could actually touch someone who had the same surgery as her husband and know he was alright. Tom didn't hesitate. "Touch it all you want," he said. "It is a little bumpy, but I am alive. I am here for my family." She asked if we wanted to see her husband and brought us back into the ICU. I couldn't believe my eyes. He was in the exact room Tom had been in during his coma. Could this really be happening? It was a surreal experience. Tom was able to relive this experience through visitors' eyes. This firefighter looked great compared to Tom, because he had fallen and hit his head and not suffered the other injuries that Tom had, but the similarities were eerie. I smiled at his wife and said "he looks great." He was cognizant and you could see in his eyes that he was there. What a healing experience to be able to give back.

A nurse at Arrowhead Regional Medical Center had brought a former brain injury patient to visit me in the ICU when Tom was still in a coma. She looked normal and functioned well in society in spite of a horrible injury. I remember looking at her and being lifted off the floor. The journey for Tom becoming normal again seemed endless and out of reach. Seeing this rehabilitated patient gave me hope. I had a glimmer of hope. Today Tom and I could be that hope for someone else.

I continued to correspond with this family and received a frantic phone call one evening from the wife asking if her children could see Tom. They were not at the hospital the day Tom and I visited, and had not received the comfort of seeing Tom. She said they were very upset and discouraged by their father's progress; seeing Tom had lifted her spirits so high, she thought it might do the same for her children. Tom was at work so I made arrangements for the family to visit the fire station. That night their three children between the ages of thirteen and nineteen came to visit Tom. When they arrived, they all hugged Tom and stared at him. I knew they were wondering if he really was okay. You always see that question in people's eyes. Like their mother, they wanted to touch Tom's scar. They asked Tom and me a million questions. It was again a privilege to help this family. They did not need our right arm, but it felt so healing to answer any questions they had. I remember the oldest son looking at Tom and smiling and he said "I can't wait to visit my dad back at work at the fire station."

Eight months after this firefighter's accident, the firefighter's wife called, sharing the good news that her husband had gone back to work. He was back driving the fire engine. What a blessing. Instead of having a brain injury patient written off and put on lifetime disability, he was back at work being a productive citizen once again.

It is my belief that God raises people to manifest His faithfulness, power, and glory. In retrospect, Tom and I were used so that God could be glorified. In our weakness He was strong in us. By telling our story of the process of deliverance from death and/or total disability, we can help others. Tom and I have been positioned to encourage and inspire others to trust God and cast their cares upon Him.

JOEL CASCADDEN:

My story is not particularly unusual. People have bad things happen to them all the time. What may be unusual is that when severely tested and overwhelmingly disappointed, I did not choose the path to victimhood.

So far, I have been tested in an extreme way twice.

My son Rick was just shy of twenty-two years when he was killed by a hit-and-run driver. This was a test. You may ask the question, what do you do? What is it like? How do you survive? I honestly do not know. But I did not become a victim. That is the point. My family and I are disappointed every day that Rick is not with us; losing a child and living with that loss. The path to becoming a victim is easy, tempting, always there.

During Tom's recovery, Joel and I talked almost daily. He was there for Tom and our family every step of the way. Joel slept on the floor of the hospital waiting room half of the first night after Tom's accident, in spite of his fractured ribs and 150 stitches. He looked awful, but I doubt the National Guard could have taken him out of the hospital. Joel knew the pain I was experiencing. I could see it in his face. I remember saying to Joel that this was the worst thing that had ever happened to me and that it could only be worse in one way and Joel knew exactly what I meant. We bonded in that pain. We talked about Rick a lot. I felt guilty that Tom had lived. Why did Tom live and Rick die? People would come into the hospital and say, "Tom, it wasn't your time; you have something left to do." When Joel was in the room, I knew he would question those comments. I would, too. We both knew we were pondering those comments but neither of us said anything.

I don't know why Tom lived and I am learning to reframe my thoughts. Tom lived and what now? We can't become victims; instead, we must give back to the world the grace, love, and compassion that we received. We could be that glimmer of hope the nurse at Arrowhead Regional Medical Center gave me that day in the ICU. It was our turn to give back. I know Joel has consoled many parents that had lost their children since Rick's death, a comfort (outside of the grace of God) that could only be given by someone who had experienced that type of pain. Again, a choice to be victorious and not a victim.

Chapter 23: *The Trial*

Being confident of this, that he who began a good work in you
will carry it on to completion until the day of Christ Jesus.
PHILIPPIANS 1:6

THE WEEKEND BEFORE THE TRIAL WAS TO BEGIN, SOUTHERN CALIfornia was on fire. It was mid-November with abnormally high temperatures and high winds sparking dangerous fires all over the southland. Tom was on duty and was placed on a strike team in Chino to protect homes that were in the path of the fire. (A strike team is a group of firefighters called out to fight fires outside of their service area.) The fires we had experienced that weekend were some of the worst in Los Angeles since the early 1960s. Over 500 homes were lost in just one of the areas in Sylmar and other fires were in Montecito, Chino Hills, Brea, and Anaheim Hills. The air was filled with smoke and I am sure that firefighters were on everyone's mind in the local area. It served as a reminder the sacrifices that firefighters made when others are in harm's way. The news had been running 24/7 commercial free throughout the weekend. It would have been impossible for anyone in southern California not to have been impacted by the tragedies our fellow Angelinos had faced over the past few days.

I had asked for some time off from work, not knowing what to expect over the next few weeks. I had stepped foot in a courtroom only one other time in my life, so the legal system was foreign to me. I had feared that the media would pick up on the trial and that a daily update would be in the local papers. But the bright side of the fires was that the local media would most likely have more important stories to cover than a trial. Tom and I had done our best to keep our kids from knowing the details of the trial. They had experienced enough tension at home and didn't need it spilling into their school life. Rebecca had started a new school that year and most of her teachers and friends were unaware of her father's accident. The last thing Tom and I wanted was for our children to have to re-live their tragedy.

A few months prior to the trial, a fellow firefighter whose child attended Catie's school asked me how we were handling the litigation. Apparently Catie had talked about it to his son, who was in her class, and the boy didn't understand why Mr. Barilla had to go to court. In a ten-year-old boy's mind, court was for criminals. He asked his father if Mr. Barilla was going to have to go to jail. As he told me the story I began to cry. It had never occurred to me how Catie may have perceived the court case. The firefighter felt awful that he had brought it up and frantically apologized for saying anything. I was so grateful that he had. It reminded me to watch my words carefully and also to explain to my children what was happening with the trial, because if I didn't, their minds would fill in the details and most likely they would receive inaccurate information from those around them.

I knew I needed to be home and available for my family during the trial. I doubt I would be any good to anyone at work anyway, as my mind would be elsewhere. I prayed that this would be the final chapter in this story and I could move on with my life. Our family needed closure and we perceived the trial as being just that.

Tom still wasn't home from the strike team the first day of the trial. Fortunately he wasn't needed, as the lawyers were working through pre-trial motions in the judge's chambers and final attempts to settle the case before going to court. The bus company had settled with the firefighters and the majority of the bus passengers prior to the trial. There were only two passengers and the bus driver left in the case.

The bus driver ended up settling the first day of court. Then only two passengers were in the mix. I have always felt that the family of the deceased deserved to be compensated. Not that money would ever bring back their loved one, but they deserved compensation, unlike others who saw this as an opportunity to make a few bucks. My prayers have been with the family of the deceased since the accident and I hope the family has found peace.

The second day of the trial continued to be full of hopes for settlement and pre-trial motions in judge's chambers. The pre-trial motions ruled not to let the CHP opinions see the light of day. The judge saw right through their bias and decided not to let them testify in the courtroom. This was a victory!

The first week of trial, or shall I say pre-trial, went so slowly. It wasn't like the movies. After day three, the court had finally ruled on all seventeen pre-trial motions. Things were looking good for us, but our defense attorney always warned not to be optimistic.

Efforts were still in full gear to settle and the judge opted to take the next two days off and begin jury selection on Monday. We were ready for this all to be over, but the waiting continued.

The next week jury selection began. Joel, his wife Lisa, Tom and I attended court all day the first day of jury selection. We sat in the courtroom all morning with the lawyers and the judge working out the logistics of the case. It was going to last a long time and the holidays were approaching quickly. Before jurors were actually chosen, they needed to be sure the jurors could commit to a month-long trial. As we sat there in the courtroom, I asked Joel if he had ever been in a courtroom before and he looked at me and said, "Yes, in fact this very room. This is the courtroom where we held the hearing for Rick's death." That was Joel's son. I closed my eyes and couldn't respond. I composed myself and asked how his wife was doing. He said he didn't know if she remembered. "How could you forget?" I replied. He said some things that hurt so bad just get tucked away so you don't have to remember. That conversation surely put the day in perspective.

The judge was methodical and thoughtful in his every action. We could not have asked for a better judge. After all of the logistics had been worked out, the first panel of potential jurors were brought into the room. As we stood upon the entry of thirty-eight potential jurors, I felt the weight of the situation begin on my heart. I looked at their faces; they were people you see at the grocery store, soccer games, or in the park. This was our community coming to judge who was at fault. Did it even matter at this point? The judge went through the timeline for the trial and asked who was unable to commit to jury duty for various reasons. It turned out that there were two firemen in the pool who knew either Tom or Joel. What were the odds? Obviously, they were excused along with twelve other potential jurors. The selection process was now in place. I asked our defense attorney, Steve Rothans, what was the point of no return? Wasn't settlement still an option? You always hear about cases settling right before trial was about to begin. Did I need to give up hope at this point? Do cases settle in the middle of trial? How did this case ever get to this point? Steve commented that opening statements were often the point of no return. Once the ship set sail, there was no stopping it.

We still had hope; the jury pool wasn't big enough to get twelve jurors and four alternates. It happened to be the week of Thanksgiving and the judge was going to be off for the rest of the week. The remaining jury pool was given a questionnaire and asked to return on the following Tuesday. The court would select another jury pool the following Monday and connect them with this pool the next day in hopes that there would be sufficient people to compose a jury.

Finally, there was a big enough jury pool. Quite a bit of time was spent deciding other issues. One lawyer was offended by a picture hanging in the courtroom of an American flag that represented 9/11. He asked the judge to consider taking it down as it gave a positive affirmation for firemen. The judge reminded the lawyer that the artwork was far less about firemen and far more about the incident and if you were to look at the twin towers the word "remember" was repeated. The other lawyers also made a motion to exclude witnesses from the courtroom. This meant Tom had to stay in the hallway. This was absolutely devastating. It was as though they tore Tom from my side again and I became very angry. Hadn't they taken him from me long enough? The jury pool rejoined us for another grueling day of juror selection, while Tom's chair sat empty in the courtroom.

On day one of week four, selection was still in process and the bus company had a clear understanding that they didn't have any friends in the jury pool, regardless of Tom's absence from the courtroom. They were anxious to settle the case, as our defense attorney Steve Rothans was increasingly confident that the case was going in our favor, even though opening statements had not yet occurred. We were scheduled to resume with jury selection after lunch that day and the bus company asked for an additional five minutes to confer with our defense attorney. Steve entered the room and whispered it was done. The case was over.

I didn't know the details, but I did know I felt as though a vice that had been closing in on me for three years and nine months had just been released. I was overwhelmed with relief. The judge entered the room and congratulated counsel for their settlement. Steve Rothans put the settlement on the record. The bus company accepted the lion's share of the liability and the city of Upland accepted about the same liability that it would have cost to try the case. It was an economical decision, but I didn't care at this point. I wanted it to be over, and it was. The jury was allowed back in the room, only to be released and given permission to talk to counsel and witnesses. Many of the potential jurors came up to Joel, Lisa, and me and said that their hearts were with us and they hoped we received what we wanted. I wanted the nightmare to be over and it was.

After the jurors left, I asked Steve if I could talk to the bus driver. He asked that I not say anything defamatory. I had the opposite in mind. I walked over and took his hand, looked him in the eye and said, "God Bless You." His eyes lit up like I had just saved his life. He smiled and feverishly shook my hand. I had just recently finished the book, *The Shack* by W.M. Paul Young, and had read about how a man had forgiven the man who killed his daughter. It was so painful to read and I knew that I had some forgiveness to do myself. Although I was no longer angry with him, this was the last step in the process. I knew if I didn't do it then, I would never have another chance. Tom said those left in the courtroom looked up in amazement. No one knew what I was going to do when I walked up to the bus driver and couldn't understand what I was saying or why I was talking to the man who almost killed my husband. I didn't have a choice. I had to forgive him so I could be free. It is true; it freed me. Forgiveness isn't for the other person who harmed you; it is for you. I haven't been the same since that moment.

The moment we walked out of the courtroom, the attorney for the bus company came up to Tom and me, shook our hands, and offered truce. He reminded us that "it wasn't personal and it was his job." We took our hands back and accepted his truce.

We celebrated that evening, but you could sense it was bittersweet for some. Had we really won a victory? Our defense attorney had prepared for battle for three-and-a-half years, only not to have to fight. Joel felt that the little liability the city of Upland agreed to was too much and was disappointed. Tom felt it was a victory because the bus company paid the majority and his family didn't have to be subjected to the stress of the trial, and he knew that it would be impossible to replicate what had happened on the freeway that day. The final outcome was just icing on the cake.

In the end, the city settled for their costs incurred by the accident and we received a handsome settlement for Tom's injuries, yet it felt like blood money. It was impossible for either of us to ever enjoy the money we received. We opted to put it all away for our children. If nothing else it could give them a financial future Tom and I never had, nor one that we ever wanted. We wanted to grow old together. God gave us that.

Chapter 24: *The New Normal*

And the God of all grace, who called you to his eternal glory in Christ, after you have suffered a little while, will himself restore you and make you strong, firm, and steadfast.
1 PETER 5:10

WHOEVER COINED THE PHRASE "THE NEW NORMAL" MUST have been in an accident or experienced serious trauma. Your old life is out the window and no matter how hard you try to get back to the day before the accident, you *never* will get there. You know what; I don't want to be there either. After all of the pain our family has experienced from this accident, in the end I am a better person because of it. I think of the old Billy Joel song that says "the good ole days weren't all that good and tomorrow ain't as bad as it seems." Tomorrow seems brighter than it has in years. God never wastes a hurt. I stopped asking why and starting using Tom's accident as an opportunity to help others. It has changed my life. Our family is no longer the victim but a victor in overcoming life's obstacles.

Tom and Dora, Christmas 2005

On April 15, 2007, exactly two years and one month after the accident Tom, the girls, and I stopped by the grocery store on our way home from church. Tom pulled right up to the store and parked so he and the girls could stay in the car while I ran in to get a few items for the week. As I was checking out, the manager frantically ran to the front of the store and someone cried, "she needs help." Instinctively, I ran to the scene and noticed a woman bleeding on the floor in obvious distress. The woman had collapsed at the entrance of the store. I turned around and motioned for Tom to come and help and to leave the kids in the car. The woman was now looking very ashen and bleeding profusely. Tom immediately took charge in providing medical assistance.

Someone came into the store and stated that she had been shot. How was this possible in a nice neighborhood on a calm Sunday morning? Wouldn't we have heard gunfire? I dismissed this notion and thought she had to be having a seizure, a heart attack, or fallen, but not a gunshot. Only moments later Tom confirmed she had been shot in the neck. Tom was the only medical professional available and continued to provide medical assistance to the now gunshot victim. He asked for paper towels to stop the bleeding while calming the woman to breathe. She began to vomit and Tom positioned her to prevent her from choking. He asked about the perpetrator, thinking about possible danger to bystanders. He asked if anyone had called 911. He made sure his family was safe. He cared for his patient with absolute professionalism. He had a command presence that was amazing. Realizing Tom had it under control, I began to pray for her healing. So many had prayed for Tom the instant they heard about the accident. I was now given the opportunity to give that back to someone in her moment of crisis. I was on my knees in the grocery store praying for a divine intervention.

The call came into the dispatcher as a gunshot victim and the sheriffs were the first emergency personnel on the scene. When they arrived, Tom continued to have control of the scene asking the sheriffs for equipment to continue life-saving techniques. He ordered a helicopter and began to breathe for the victim. Tom explained that he was a paramedic and the sheriffs allowed him to continue to provide medical care. They could obviously see he had control of the situation and knew the paramedics might be a while. It took about seven minutes for the paramedics to arrive; they were gearing up in their flack jackets before coming on scene. Appropriately so, after all, there was a gunshot victim in a grocery store and the perpetrator had not yet been apprehended. Tom continued to help the paramedics until the victim was loaded into the ambulance and taken to the helicopter that had since landed at the park next door. The victim was airlifted to Arrowhead Regional Medical Center. Our car was taped off in a crime scene and we were asked to stay and give witness statements. I called my friend Jill and asked her to pick up Catie and Rebecca because Tom and I were needed at the scene to make statements.

While we waited for the police to take our statements, I listened to the bystanders thank Tom for his actions. "If you hadn't have been there that woman would have died;" "You were great;" "Thank God you were there to save her."

I know Tom provides life-saving techniques to people everyday in his job, but to be positioned off duty to perform those duties is a different story altogether. As I sat and listened to the bystanders give Tom praise, I thought about the scene of Tom's accident: how people had provided immediate attention and saved his life. It felt good to be able to help this woman in her hour of need. It was an opportunity to give back a fraction of what was given to us.

Barilla Family

Later that evening my nine-year-old daughter Catie mentioned she was concerned that this happened so close to her home. She said that these things usually happened far away and it was scary that it happened so close. Tom's response was unexpected. Tom said "Catie, we should be grateful that we live in a community where so many people came out to help someone who was in danger." He was right. Both the store employees and the customers immediately went to help. Tom asked for paper towels and scissors and he had about five pairs of scissors within seconds. Everyone knew she had been shot and the shooter had not been caught, yet people responded unselfishly because it was the right thing to do. It was exactly what had been done the morning of March 15, 2005. Thanks to the quick response of the people on the freeway that day, Tom was not only alive, but he was available to help save the life of the gunshot victim two years later.

I have always been intrigued by reciprocity. God not only saved Tom, but saved him with a purpose. Really understanding that concept took away the longing to get back to the day before the accident. Perhaps the new normal was not so bad. To live a life with meaning and purpose may have come at the cost of a long painful journey. That morning in the grocery store provided incredible insight to the healing process. It made me want to share my journey with others. Why was Tom's recovery a miracle? It is not a secret. Appropriate medical attention is important, but it is not the only tools we had in our journey. It was our faith, our love, and the support we received from the community that allowed Tom a miraculous recovery.

EXCERPT FROM AN EMAIL SENT TO HER FRIENDS AND FAMILY FROM THE WOMAN WHO WAS SHOT.

Dearest Ohana, (Ohana = family in Hawaiian)

This past Friday night I met with Tom and his family. It is hard to digest everything that Tom (firefighter/Angel) and Dora (Angel/ wife) told me about what happened when they discovered me in Vons but the bottom line is by the time I hit the floor in Vons I had run out of oxygen and Tom had to breathe for me. He then stabilized me and got the paramedics, helicopter and police organized. He made sure that I never lost my pulse which meant that I could be airlifted. This was a divine appointment; make no mistake. I wrote him after the dinner and thanked him for not slacking on his rehab because had he not been there to breathe for me, I am sure I would have had brain damage or would have died.

A year ago today I was on my third hospital and hating every minute of it. I felt lonely and like I was in prison. I also felt like they wanted me to be there longer than necessary; this was of course not reality. Today Mom is with me again and we are packing to go to Europe, I can not only breathe, eat, and speak but I have gone back to work. The blessings just don't seem to stop. My life isn't without its ups and downs but when I think of where I was last year compared to today I don't even dare complain. Thank you for letting me share my thoughts with all of you and I truly hope this blesses you and others around you.

Love, Teri

I have often wondered why Tom survived; was it to save Teri? To be there for me and the girls? Why? Is he supposed to do something amazing in the future and God needed him to stay alive? I have come to the conclusion it is not healthy to ask why but to bask in the blessings I have been given and use them to bless others. My life is forever changed and it is a new day. I have also come to realize that healing begins with understanding that God is in control and we are part of His sovereign plan.

The proceeds of this book will be donated to help trauma and brain injury patients.
Please join me in giving to families what was given to Tom and I during our healing journey.
Partners for Better Health (PBH) is an IRS 501(c)(3) charitable organization.
Please send checks made payable to
Partners for Better Health, 215 W. C Street, Ontario, CA 91762.

Dora Barilla